BONNIE PRINCE CHARLIE

BONNIE PRINCE CHARLIE

ROSALIND K. MARSHALL

NATIONAL MUSEUMS OF SCOTLAND
NATIONAL GALLERIES OF SCOTLAND
NATIONAL LIBRARY OF SCOTLAND
HISTORIC BUILDINGS AND MONUMENTS (SDD)

EDINBURGH: HER MAJESTY'S STATIONERY OFFICE

Designed by HMSO Graphic Design

HMSO publications are available from:

HMSO Bookshops
71 Lothian Road, Edinburgh EH3 9AZ   (031) 228 4181
49 High Holborn, London WC1V 6HB   (01) 211 5656 (Counter service only)
258 Broad Street, Birmingham B1 2HE   (021) 643 3740
Southey House, 33 Wine Street, Bristol BS1 2BQ   (0272) 24306/24307
9-21 Princess Street, Manchester M60 8AS   (061) 834 7201
80 Chichester Street, Belfast BT1 4JY   (0232) 234488

HMSO Publications Centre
(Mail and telephone orders only)
PO Box 276, London SW8 5DT
Telephone orders (01) 622 3316
General enquiries (01) 211 5656

HMSO's Accredited Agents
(see Yellow Pages)

And through good booksellers

Printed in Scotland for HMSO by Lithoprint (Scotland) Ltd.
Dd. 287127/HF4690   C120   3/88

ISBN 0 11 493420 7

CONTENTS

ACKNOWLEDGMENTS

I should like to thank the owners of all the items included as illustrations in this book, particularly Historic Buildings and Monuments (SDD) and the Trustees of the National Galleries of Scotland, the National Library of Scotland and the National Museums of Scotland. The willing co-operation of these institutions has been much appreciated. Individual acknowledgments will be found in the captions.

Professor Gordon Donaldson, HM Historiographer in Scotland, and John S Gibson kindly commented on the completed text, Mr Gibson generously discussing with me the most recent research into the Prince's wanderings after Culloden. The following friends and colleagues gave valuable assistance: Gavin Turner, Alastair Cherry, Charles Burnett, Dr David Breeze, Dr Ewan Scott, Fabio Bruscaglioni, George Dalgleish, Dr David Caldwell, Edward and Minnie Haman, Colonel Donald Wickes and James Holloway. I am grateful to them all.

RKM
Edinburgh, September 1987

NOTE ON NAMES AND DATES

When James II died in exile in 1701, his supporters had his son proclaimed King of Great Britain. For Jacobites, he always was King James III of England and VIII of Scotland. In the interests of brevity, I have called him James III, the title by which he would doubtless have been known had he been restored to the throne after the Union of 1707.

The Prince always signed his own name simply as 'Charles' so that is the form I have used. Incidentally, 'Charlie' when applied to him was not the English diminutive but the way the Gaelic word for Charles, *Tearlach*, was pronounced.

As for dates, during the first half of the eighteenth century Britain followed the Old Style Julian calendar while France and other Roman Catholic countries used the New Style Gregorian calendar. This meant that British dates were ten days behind. Following the usual practice, I have used Old Style when the Prince was in Britain, New Style when he was on the continent, and I have indicated in the text where the changes take place. In 1752 the problem was solved because Britain adopted the New Style.

Finally, I have translated quotations from French into English and I have modernised spelling and punctuation. All direct speech which I have quoted has been taken from the recollections of those people who were present at the time. The principal sources will be found in the note on further reading.

1

THE PRINCE'S PARENTS

IN THE spring of 1718, a young Irish soldier arrived at the Palace of Ohlau in Silesia. Charles Wogan had come to see Prince James Sobieski on a very delicate mission. For some weeks past he had been travelling round Germany in search of a wife for his royal master, King James III of Great Britain, but so far he had met with no success. The Catholic princesses he had seen were either too fat, too old or too ugly. Perhaps this time he would be more fortunate.

Presenting his letter of introduction, he was admitted to the presence of the Prince, who welcomed him with some enthusiasm. It might be thirty years now since the Stuarts had lost the British throne, King James III might have lived almost all his life in exile, but Roman Catholics throughout Europe still supported his cause. Even after this long interval there were many who believed that it was simply a matter of time before he would regain his rightful inheritance. A glittering future could await the lady he chose to be his bride. The Polish Prince was therefore ready to agree that Wogan could spend a few weeks in the palace getting to know his daughters.

The Sobieska girls certainly looked promising. Their ancestry was impeccable. Their grandfather had been the heroic warrior King of Poland who had driven back the Turks from the gates of Vienna. One of their cousins was Holy Roman Emperor, another was King of Portugal and the Pope was the godfather of the youngest daughter. The family were faithful Catholics and they were also wealthy: one glance at their sumptuously furnished palace was enough to confirm that.

In theory, any of the three sisters would make a suitable bride for the King, but Charles Wogan was perceptive enough to realise that temperament mattered too. James would not be an easy man to please. His life so far had been one long series of disappointments. Ever since his father's death when he himself was just thirteen he had devoted himself to regaining the lost throne. Time and again, military and naval expeditions had set off for Britain, only to end in failure. Twice, he had gone himself. The first time he was not even able to set foot in his kingdom. The second time, he found himself embroiled in the disaster of the 1715 campaign. It was hardly surprising that his early enthusiasm had been replaced by gloomy resignation. 'I was born under an unlucky star', he would say mournfully and it was becoming increasingly difficult to rouse him from his depression. That was why his friends were so anxious that he should marry. With the right wife and the prospect of sons to carry on his name he would surely take heart once more.

Inspecting the Sobieska sisters with a shrewd and critical eye, Wogan saw at once that Casimire, the eldest, would never do. Raised

1. *James III*, soon after his marriage, probably painted by F. Trevisani. (Scottish National Portrait Gallery)

2. *Charles Wogan,*
James III's emissary, by an
unknown Irish artist.
(National Gallery of
Ireland)

by an elderly grandmother, she had grown up to be an 'astonishingly serious' young lady, obsessed with the details of court etiquette. If she married James, the pair of them would sink into the depths of despondency together. She was obviously unsuitable.

Charlotte, the second daughter, was the exact opposite. High-spirited and playful, thoughtless and heedless, she would grate on the King's nerves, irritating him with her over-familiarity and her endless jokes. 'One who has suffered his troubles is not always in the mood to appreciate humour', Wogan remarked sagely, and he rejected her.

That left Clementina, the youngest: sweet, innocent, thoughtful, discreet, altogether enchanting Clementina. She was exactly what James needed. She was biddable, eager to please and as pretty as a picture, with delicate features and large, dark eyes. Admittedly, she was tiny, and so thin that she seemed almost fragile, but her eager parents insisted that she would grow yet: after all, she was only fifteen.

Wogan was doubtful but his reservations were swept away by a most extraordinary coincidence. Listening to her laughing and chattering to her sisters, he heard them address her as 'Queen of England'. What could it mean? His purpose in coming to the castle had been kept secret from the princesses. They thought that he was simply a pleasant foreign gentleman visiting the area. He had to find out more and an obliging courtier was ready to enlighten him. When the girls were small, he explained, they had played at being grown-up ladies and they had selected exotic titles for themselves. Clementina had liked the sound of 'Queen of England' and that had been her family nickname ever since.

3. *Clementina Sobieska*, painted about 1720, probably by F. Trevisani. (Scottish National Portrait Gallery)

It was a good omen. Wogan at once spoke to Prince Sobieski, who declared himself delighted with the match. He then approached Clementina. She was thrilled. Well pleased, he was able to sit down and write an enthusiastic letter to James in Bologna telling him that he had found him the ideal wife.

The King was hardly the most eager bridegroom in the world, but he knew that he must marry and he was prepared to rely on Wogan's judgment. Messengers rode back and forth between Italy and Ohlau. The marriage contract was signed and Clementina's godfather, the Pope, was so pleased that he offered to increase her dowry. The wedding date was set and the Princess and her mother began to assemble the trousseau. At that point, a characteristically dampening message arrived from James III. He was in mourning for his mother, he wrote, and so 'a simple white dress will suffice for the ceremony'.

4. *George I*, in 1716, by
G. Kneller.
(National Portrait Gallery,
London)

However depressing this instruction might seem, it failed to quench
their excitement.

Much more serious was his other warning. The whole marriage plan
must be kept strictly secret, he said, for whatever else happened,
George I must not get wind of it. The last thing George wanted was
James marrying and having children. That would pose a dangerous
threat to the Hanoverian monarchy in Britain. 'He will move heaven
and earth to hinder it' said James, and so they must delay no longer.
The Princess must set out at once, telling no one where she was going.

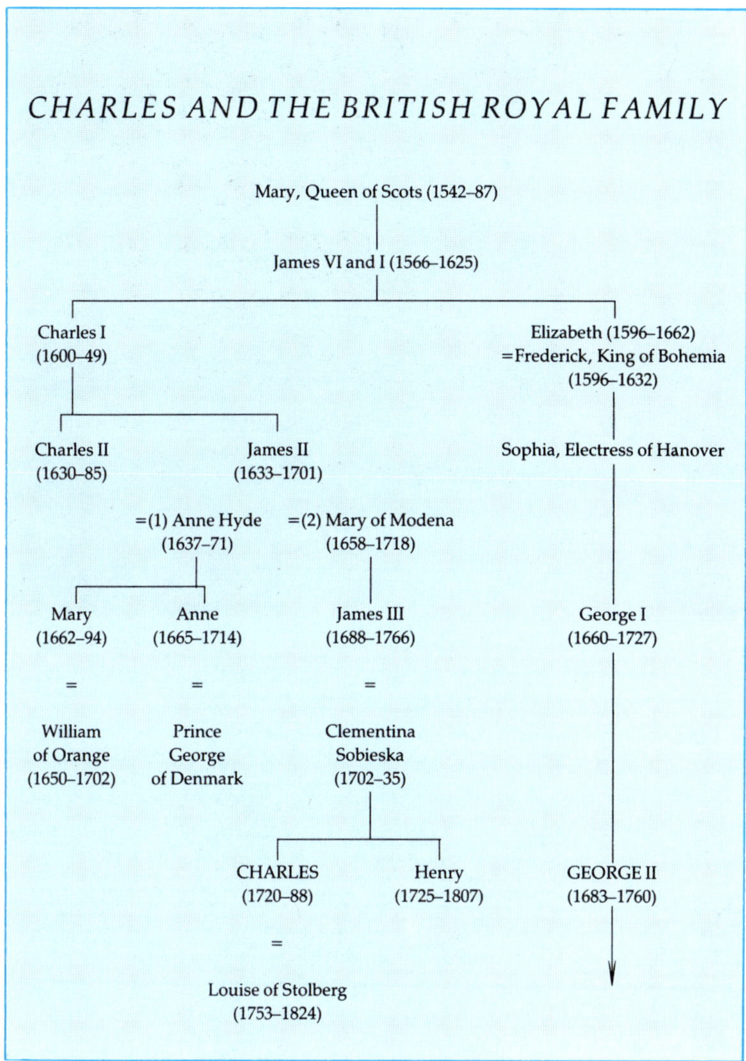

Urged on by Prince Sobieski, who was determined not to lose such an eligible son-in-law, Clementina and her mother swallowed their disappointment at being deprived of a lavish wedding, announced that they were going on a pilgrimage and set off for Italy. They had travelled as far as Innsbruck when the blow fell. The Emperor decreed that they were to be placed under house arrest. Somehow or other his friend George I had found out about the marriage and had sent him a letter indicating in no uncertain terms that if he valued their alliance he would not let the ceremony take place.

Clementina was horrified, her mother was distraught and her father was furious. Even James received the news with something less than his accustomed calm. He went so far as to write his bride a series of indignant and encouraging letters, but all too soon he became convinced that fate, as usual, was against him. Clementina was not for

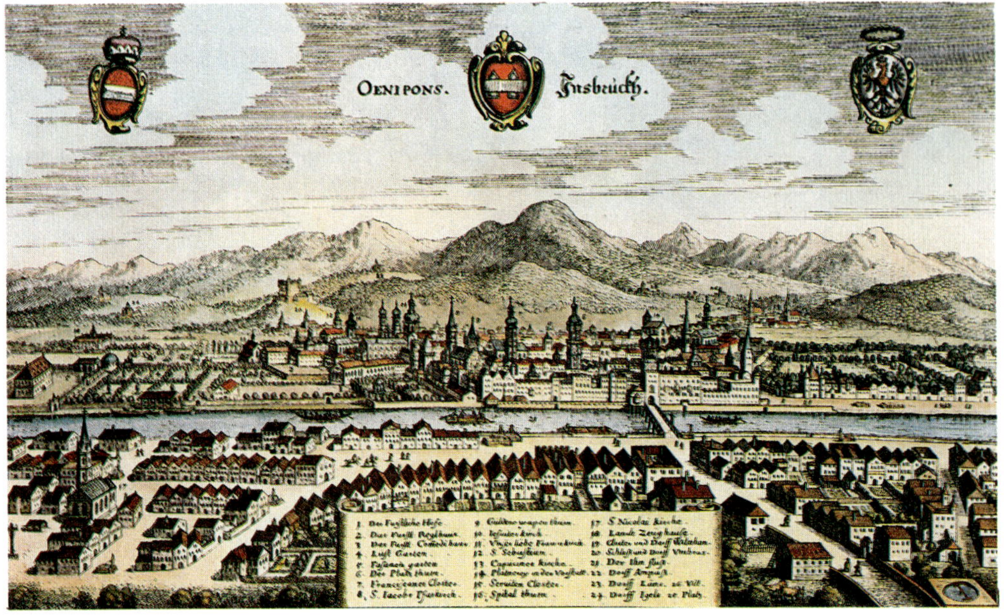

5. Innsbruck in the seventeenth century, engraved by M. Merian. (From *Topographia Austriae,* 1649)

him. He ordered his agents to look for a substitute. Perhaps Maria di Capraro, the local heiress, would do instead.

Not everyone was so ready to accept defeat. Charles Wogan decided that he could not possibly allow matters to end thus. After all his trouble, after his splendid discovery of the perfect bride, he could not bear to see his careful plans collapse. He would go to Innsbruck and snatch Clementina from the clutches of her captors.

James gave his reluctant consent. With the prospect of the marriage fading rapidly, he had already turned his mind to matters of greater moment. A new invasion of Britain was being planned by the Spaniards. He would go to Madrid himself to see what was happening. Wogan could do what he pleased.

Nothing could be done for the time being, for it was winter now, and the passes between Italy and Austria were blocked by snow. As soon as the better weather came, however, Wogan set off for Innsbruck, disguised as a merchant. First of all he persuaded the Emperor's officials to let him visit the Princess, and then he rode on to Ohlau to consult her father. After that, he gathered together a little band of Irish friends who would help him in his daring scheme. There was his uncle, Captain Gaydon, his friend Captain O'Toole, who was a fluent German speaker, and a fellow officer, Captain Misset. Mrs Misset insisted on going along as well. The others tried to dissuade her, for she was several months pregnant, but she declared that the Princess would need her there as a chaperone. Apart from that, her maid, Jenny, was to play a vital part in the proceedings. Together they hired a coach and travelled to Innsbruck.

It was late April now, but still bitterly cold, with snow lying deep on the streets. Even so, they were all in a mood of high good humour.

Failure could mean imprisonment, even death, but they were determined not to fail. Come what may, they would rescue the Princess. At 11.30 on the night of 27th April* Wogan smuggled Jenny into the mansion where Clementina was held, and there, in the privacy of the Princess's bedchamber, she and the maid changed clothes. Muffled up in a threadbare cloak, Clementina then crept downstairs and out into the black, moonless night, a blizzard swirling around her. Back inside, Jenny climbed into her bed and pulled the covers up over her head, praying that she would not be discovered until morning. What would happen then, she dared not think.

Meanwhile, the Princess hurried along the street to the corner where Wogan was waiting for her. Together they floundered through the snow to a nearby inn where the others had gathered. Everyone exclaimed in dismay at the sight of Clementina's drenched and bedraggled figure, but she only laughed and allowed Mrs Misset to take her into the next room and help her into dry clothes. Comfortable and warm though it was in the inn, they dared not linger. At any moment Jenny might be discovered. As soon as the Princess was ready they hurried outside, climbed into the coach and set off on the long road across the Alps to Italy.

It was dreadfully cold, they were in terror of being pursued by the Emperor's men and Clementina was suddenly overcome by the enormity of what she was doing, but Captain Misset was 'a great comedian' and he kept them all in fits of laughter with his jokes and imitations. His wife was equally entertaining. Not to be outdone, she had a fund of amusing anecdotes about theatres she had visited and plays she had seen. Her spirits reviving, Clementina began to ask a thousand questions about James, his court and the British way of life.

The miles sped by almost unnoticed, but as they reached the top of the Brenner Pass, the reaction to all the excitement set in, the Princess turned pale and suddenly she fainted. For one horrible moment her companions thought she was dead, but Mrs Misset produced a bottle of smelling-salts, waved it under Clementina's nose and chafed her cold hands. With a sigh the Princess came back to life, opening her eyes to laugh weakly at the anxious expressions on the faces of her friends. They looked for all the world like worried monkeys, she said, and their obvious concern seemed to give her new strength.

'Take courage, it is nothing!' she told them, and when she had sipped a little wine she pronounced herself fit to proceed.

The worst of the weather was over now and as they descended the southern slopes of the Alps they found themselves entering a mild and welcome spring. The alarms of the journey were far from past, though. There was a terrifying incident when they almost collided with another coach on a narrow, twisting road above a precipice, and a new crisis awaited them when they reached the town of Trent. Wilting in the heat of her ermine-lined dress, Clementina hoped to stop at an inn to change into something cooler. Before she could alight, however, it was

---

* New Style

6. Medal commemorating Clementina's escape from Innsbruck. She is shown in a carriage with Rome in the background and the motto, 'I follow his fortune and his cause'.
(National Museums of Scotland)

discovered that a German prince who knew her family well was also passing through the town. Terrified that she would be recognised, Clementina crouched down out of sight on the floor of the coach for almost four hours. Her friends were hardly surprised when she grew pale once more. Mrs Misset hastily produced the smelling-salts and pointed out that the Princess had scarcely eaten since leaving Innsbruck. Nourishment was what she needed.

They managed to find a wayside inn and persuaded her to take a little tea and a piece of bread. She refused everything else with the sweet firmness they were beginning to recognise. Inadequate though the meal might seem, it restored her, which was just as well. An hour or two later the axle-tree of their coach snapped and it would take a good deal of time to repair. The only replacement to be had was a two-wheeled, open farm-cart. Undaunted, Clementina and Mrs Misset climbed aboard, laughing and joking. In this unconventional mode of transport the King of Poland's granddaughter entered Italy at 2 o'clock on the morning of Sunday, 30 April 1719.

Happily, the rest of the journey proved to be relatively uneventful. They reached Verona without incident and on 2 May they finally arrived at Bologna, only to discover that James III was still in Spain. That was a sad disappointment, and tiresome too, for it meant that Clementina would have to keep her identity secret. She might be out of reach of the Emperor's soldiers in Italy, but there were always spies and foreign agents and she must take no risks until her marriage was safely accomplished.

A week passed. The Princess recovered from the journey, bought herself some much-needed new clothes and did a little sightseeing. Many of the great local families were away from home but it was possible to look round their palaces. She particularly asked to be shown over the Capraro Palace, so Captain Gaydon escorted her. She gazed eagerly at all she saw and he thought she was simply interested in comparing it with her own house at Ohlau, but then they came upon a portrait of Maria di Capraro, the daughter of the family, and the lady James had considered marrying instead. They had thought that the Princess knew nothing about that, but when he glanced at her covertly, Gaydon noticed that she had 'flushed vermilion' and he concluded that she was perfectly well aware of James's search for a substitute.

Fortunately, there was not much more time for idle gossip and speculation, because on 9 May a special message arrived from James III. The Spanish invasion plan had fallen through, the King intended to come back to Italy and in the meantime a proxy wedding ceremony must be arranged. The bearers of this reassuring message were a Scottish couple of some influence in the Royal Household: James Murray and his sister, Mrs Marjorie Hay.

Mr Murray was a handsome young man, still under thirty, with a long nose and bright, alert eyes. The son of a Scottish nobleman, he had qualified in law but he had never actually practised. Instead, he had embraced the Jacobite cause and had come to Italy to serve

James III. He rose rapidly in the Royal Household and soon he was one of the King's most trusted advisers. That did not please his fellow exiles. They were jealous, of course, but apart from that it was his manner that people found so objectionable. He 'gave himself airs', the Jacobite nobles complained, and they considered him both arrogant and patronising. Clementina disliked him on sight.

His sister was rather more acceptable. She was disconcertingly like him in appearance, but in her, his somewhat sardonic air was transmuted into a sprightly friendliness, and if she seemed a trifle bold, at least she was affable. She announced that she was to be the Princess's lady-in-waiting. Moreover, she would begin her duties at once for the proxy wedding would take place the very next day, with Mr Murray standing in for the bridegroom.

On the morning of 10 May 1719 Clementina therefore put on her simple white dress with a plain white cap and the fabulous Sobieski pearls. She made her confession, took communion and was married

7. *James Murray*, who stood proxy for James III at his wedding, by F. Trevisani.
(In a Scottish private collection)

with the special ring James had sent for the purpose. Oblivious of the unfavourable impression he had made upon the bride, Mr Murray wrote to tell a friend, 'God be thanked, Her Majesty is in perfect health after a most fatiguing journey in very bad weather, and if beauty, virtue, good sense and good nature be sufficient to make our Master happy in a Queen, I dare say she possesses them to an eminent degree'.

They set off for Rome that very afternoon, after some unseemly wrangling. The plan had been that Clementina should travel with Mr Murray and Mrs Hay. When she discovered that Charles Wogan and his friends had been told to go about their business, she was furious. She would not set out at all unless they went with her, she announced. A special bond had developed between the new Queen and her gallant rescuers and she could not bear to see them being shabbily treated. Apart from that, she was feeling nervous of the new life ahead of her,

and she longed for their reassuring company. Confronted with an unexpectedly stubborn and rebellious Clementina, Mr Murray gave in and said that they should all go along together. As they travelled south, the Queen deliberately took her meals with Wogan and the others, and a merry time they had of it, giggling, reminiscing, making private jokes and dissolving into helpless laughter whenever the irrepressible Captain Misset did his imitation of Mr Murray.

This lighthearted frivolity could not go on indefinitely, of course, and on 16 May they made a state entry into Rome, welcomed by huge, cheering crowds. Everyone had heard about Clementina's epic journey and they were entranced at the sight of this pretty, graceful young girl who had risked all manner of dangers for the sake of her future husband. James III's household were desperate to meet her, and so it was doubly galling to them when Mr Murray announced that, in the King's absence, she was to stay in the utmost privacy in an Ursuline convent, seeing no one except a select few whom he himself would admit.

The Jacobite lords and ladies were furious. An exiled court was not a happy place at the best of times and James III's followers were continually arguing and quarrelling with each other. Disappointed, insecure, deprived of their lands and their rightful role in life, they spent their empty days fuming and raging over matters both great and small. They blamed each other for the failure of the 1715 rising, they suspected each other of being Hanoverian spies and they were

constantly alert for any favour, real or imagined, conferred upon any of their number by the King.

They all criticised the Duke of Mar for his appalling lack of leadership in 1715, the Duke spent his time making trouble for the Earl of Panmure, and Lord Pitsligo was convinced that he was being ruined by his rivals. The Catholics fell out with the Protestants, the Scots quarrelled with the Irish and the old nobility resented those awarded titles more recently. If they agreed on anything, it was their hatred of the obnoxious Mr Murray, and now they were united in their condemnation of what they saw as his unwarranted interference.

Clementina was upset too. Shut away in her convent, she was longing to meet everyone and take her rightful place in the world. Bored and frustrated, she announced that she would set off for Spain to meet her husband. The Pope hastily put a stop to that foolish scheme, and to calm the situation Mr Murray was persuaded to let her see her future household. The lords and ladies were temporarily mollified, their attention diverted by the sight of their new mistress. She was, they decided, entirely satisfactory, and the Scottish Countess

of Nithsdale spoke for them all when she described her as 'one of the charmingest, obliging and well bred young ladies that ever was seen. Our Master cannot but be extremely happy in her, and all those who has the good fortune to have any dependence on her. To add to it, she is very pretty, has good eyes, a fine skin, well-shaped for her height, but is not tall, but may be so yet, for she is but seventeen and looks even younger'.

It only remained for her to meet her bridegroom, and at long last the moment came. James was on his way. He still wanted a quiet wedding, so he sent word that Clementina was to travel to Montefiascone about seventy miles north of Rome. Needless to say, Mrs Hay was to chaperone her, but she was allowed an escort of Charles Wogan, Captain Misset and the others. Only Mrs Misset had to stay behind, having recently given birth to her child.

Arriving at Montefiascone, Clementina met James for the first time in a room in the Bishop's Palace. If her romantic imagination had conjured up a handsome picture of the King, she was not disappointed. She saw before her a tall, imposing man with a large, aquiline nose and

11. *James, 4th Earl of Panmure*, painted before his exile from Scotland, probably by John Scougall. (On loan to the Scottish National Portrait Gallery from the Earl of Mar and Kellie: photograph, *Scotland's Story*)

heavy, sombre eyes. Everyone who met him commented upon his distinguished presence, his manner, regal yet gracious, and his strong resemblance to his father and his uncle, James II and Charles II. He was every inch a king.

For his part, James was definitely taken with Clementina. Soon he was writing enthusiastically about her to all his friends. 'In the midst of my misfortune', he said, 'I can count myself the happiest man in the world.' His bride had surpassed all his expectations. She was pretty, polite, nicely dressed and, best of all, it seemed to him that she had 'not so much as a will of her own'.

The marriage took place on 1 September in the hall of the Bishop's Palace, where an altar had been set up with a silken kneeler before it. The Bishop himself officiated, addressing the couple in French.

When the vows had been exchanged, he ceremoniously blessed their bedchamber, and then there was a magnificent banquet, during which James graciously knighted Charles Wogan, Captain Misset, Captain O'Toole and Captain Gaydon. After that, they all went to the cathedral to hear an oratorio.

Truly married at last, James and his wife were both eager to settle down in Rome. Hitherto, the King had possessed no home there, but now the Pope gave him the Muti Palace in the Street of the Holy Apostles. A stately, four-storey building some sixty years old, it was plain but handsome in appearance and inside there was a pleasant little courtyard. Clementina was particularly pleased because it was so

12. *The Marriage of James III and Clementina*, painted by A. Masucci for James, who presented it to the Bishop who performed the ceremony.
(Scottish National Portrait Gallery)

13. Medal commemorating the marriage of James and Clementina, 1719.
(National Museums of Scotland)

close to the Church of the Holy Apostles and she resolved to go to Mass there every day.

Her religion was the one reassuringly familiar feature of an otherwise alien way of life. James III had long since established in his household a routine which he believed to be utterly British, or, to be more precise, English. Although he was half Italian and had spent only his first few weeks in Britain, he regarded himself as being completely English. He dressed in English clothes, wrote and spoke English as his native language and ate English food. Roast beef appeared regularly on his dining table in Rome. He had an immense admiration for the English character and he was determined that when he finally returned to his true home his subjects would detect in him no trace of foreignness. The likelihood of that ever really happening was becoming increasingly remote but, surrounded as he was by wistful exiles, he had to go on trying.

There was a new spirit of optimism now in James's household, thanks to the presence of Clementina. She was still the sensation of Roman society. All the aristocracy flocked to see her and she, with her deep love of music, delighted in going to operas and concerts as well as to balls. Everyone wanted to hear about her adventures on her journey south, and she never tired of telling them.

Revelling in the attention, she scarcely had time to notice that the King was not quite the ardent husband of her imaginings. He spent long hours shut away in his study with Mr Murray and Mrs Hay's dull husband, and when he did emerge, he was inclined to treat his wife with a rather condescending kindliness. He was a reserved man, distant and reluctant to show his emotions. His Scottish supporters had disliked his chilly manner when he had visited their kingdom and

14. The Muti Palace in Rome, where Charles was born and brought up. (Bibliotheca Hertziana, Max-Planck Institut, Rome)

15. *Winifred, Countess of Nithsdale*, painted before she left Scotland by J. B. Medina.
(By kind permission of Peter Maxwell Stuart of Traquair House, Innerleithen, Peeblesshire)

16. *John Hay*, James III's close adviser. This roundel from his tomb in Avignon is the only known portrait of him.
(Photograph in Scottish National Portrait Gallery Archive)

Clementina had just begun to find it irritating when an exciting new development took up her attention. She decided that she was pregnant. The baby would be born in October 1720, she announced.

At once, she found herself at the centre of an ecstatic wave of enthusiasm. Indeed, it seemed that the whole of Western Europe was enthralled by the news. Suddenly, Jacobitism seemed to be a viable proposition again, a very real threat to the Hanoverian monarchy of Britain. The Stuart dynasty could be ignored no longer. Political implications apart, there was immense personal satisfaction in the Muti Palace and, of course, a whole new round of squabbling broke out among the courtiers. Mrs Hay had been the first to know: Mrs Hay, of all people – a woman who had never borne a child. Lady Nithsdale and the other oft-confined mothers stormed and raged, but as autumn came their indignation turned to bewilderment. October passed but there was no baby. November came and went and on 10 December a puzzled Mrs Hay was confiding to her husband, 'Her Majesty grows bigger every day – but I believe we shall not get our Prince before New Year'. She and Clementina had somehow miscalculated. Not surprising, the ladies told each other smugly, in view of their inexperience in such matters.

Frustrating though it was, no one was unduly worried, for the Queen was in excellent health. To console her for her tedious wait, the Pope blessed four candles and sent them to the Muti Palace with instructions that they were to be lit when her labour began. He also

17. The Church of the Holy Apostles, near the Muti Palace, where Clementina went to Mass each day.
(Bibliotheca Hertziana, Max-Planck Institut, Rome)

18. Medal commemorating the birth of Prince Charles in 1720. The column denotes the fortitude of the exiled Stuarts and the globe shows the countries claimed by them. (National Museums of Scotland)

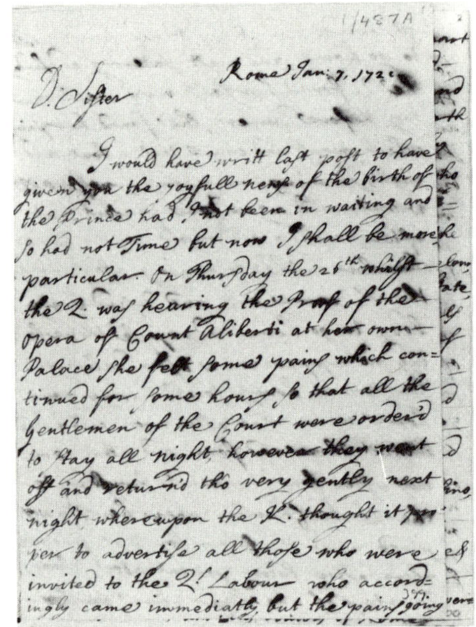

19. Letter from Winifred, Countess of Nithsdale, describing the birth of Charles. (Abercairny Papers, Scottish Record Office. Reproduced by kind permission of W. G. Drummond Moray Esq)

sent her a valuable Chinese statue and a complete set of extremely expensive baby clothes. Not to be outdone, one of the cardinals presented her with a sumptuous crimson velvet cloak lined with lynx fur, a gift to him from no less a personage than the Czar of Russia. Basking in the attention, Clementina found that her every whim was indulged and she even managed to arrange for her favourite opera company to rehearse in her apartments so that she need not miss their latest performance.

Christmas came. She was still in the best of health. The festivities went off without incident, but the following afternoon, while she was listening to the singers, she felt a sudden pain. The baby must be coming at last. She called out to her ladies and immediately the entire household was thrown into a flurry of activity. The midwife was already on the premises, of course. Indeed, she had practically become a permanent feature of the household. Other people had to be summoned as well, however.

The contractions were very slow at first, so the King counselled patience, but on the following morning he sent out his invitations to over a hundred carefully chosen guests. Italian princes and princesses, cardinals and bishops, ambassadors and administrators, and British lords and ladies came flocking to the palace, there to be shown into the large antechamber adjoining the Queen's room. They were to perform a special function. They would witness the birth, and then they would carry to the outside world the news that the King had a child, a real, royal child, not a substitute or changeling.

All that afternoon they waited and all evening too. At ten o'clock the communicating door opened and they found the King regarding them morosely. They should go home and rest, he said. The Queen's pains

had stopped and the birth was obviously not imminent. Next morning Clementina was up and about as though nothing were happening. On Sunday she was in the best of spirits, but on Monday, just before dinner, she gave a sudden cry of alarm. The contractions had begun again.

Out went the messengers, back came the cardinals, the bishops, the lords and the ladies. Excitedly they trooped up to the antechamber and settled down to wait. Slowly the night went past. Morning came. At nine o'clock the communicating door opened and the King emerged. They should go home and rest, he said, for the delivery would not take place for several hours yet.

Muttering and grumbling, they tramped down the steps, along the Street of the Holy Apostles and back to their own palaces, where they climbed gladly into bed. Just after three o'clock that afternoon they were aroused by a hammering at their doors. The baby was about to arrive. Wearily they made their way once more to the palace, up the long flight of steps, and into the all too familiar antechamber, but this time they did not have long to wait. At about twenty-five past four, the communicating door swung open and they were invited inside.

Clementina was seated in a birthing chair by her bed, her midwife bending over her and her husband hovering nearby. It was evident from her sharp cries that the birth was indeed imminent and sure enough, at ten past five, 'she at last brought forth a child', Lady Nithsdale noted, 'which was accompanied by the loud huzzas of all

20. *Charles in his swaddling clothes*, being admired by the Jacobite court, by L. Sconzani.
(Bologna State Archives)

21. *The Baptism of Prince Charles*, painted by A. Masucci and P. L. Ghezzi for James III, who presented it to the officiating Bishop. (Scottish National Portrait Gallery)

the bystanders'. Triumphantly the midwife held up the baby for everyone to see, shouting in rapturous tones, 'See! Here is no impostor! Behold, a real Prince is born!'

Captain Misset's wife, now Lady Misset, had been appointed as lady-in-waiting to the new arrival and she hastily snatched the infant away. She bore him into the next room, followed by the jostling and pushing notabilities. There, they were able to reassure themselves that the baby really was a boy, and a fine, large, healthy boy at that. King James III of Great Britain had his son and heir.

The guns of the Castle Saint Angelo boomed out over the city to announce his birth. People sang and danced in the streets and there were loud cries of 'Long live the Prince!' As darkness fell, bonfires were kindled, fireworks exploded and ecclesiastical palaces were illuminated. Some Jacobites even claimed that a new star had appeared in the sky.

Inside the palace, the King gave orders for the immediate baptism of his son. The Bishop of Montefiascone, who had married James to Clementina, had the honour of christening the baby in the Queen's private chapel. He was given the names Charles Edward Louis John Casimir Silvester Xavier Maria. His father would call him by the Italian diminutive Carluccio, his mother would address him with the Polish Carluso and to history he would be known as Bonnie Prince Charlie.

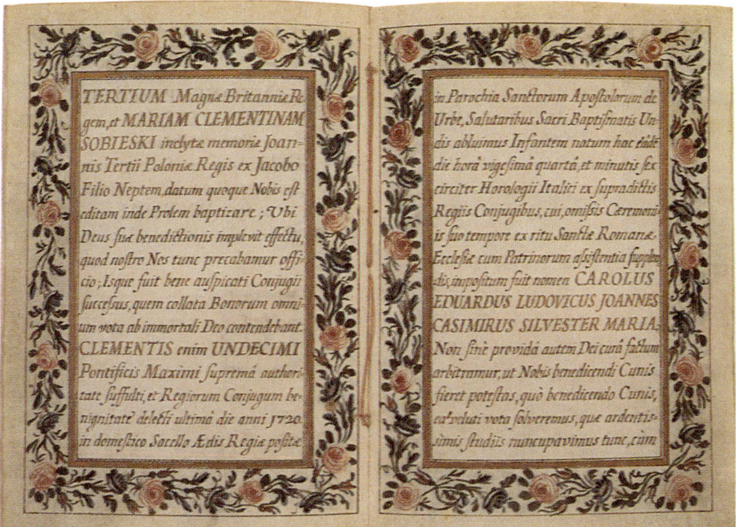

22. Baptismal certificate of the Prince, with his full name on the second page. The final page, not shown, has the signature and seal of the Bishop of Montefiascone. (National Library of Scotland)

2

A ROMAN CHILDHOOD

*A*S SOON as his christening was over, Lady Misset carried the baby through to the new royal nurseries, where the excited staff were waiting to take care of him. The King had insisted that the women employed there should be British. In charge was Mrs Hughes, who seems to have come from Wales, and her helpers were all fellow exiles. The only exception was the wet-nurse. Queens did not feed their own children, of course. A nursing mother was hired for the purpose. On this occasion, no one suitable could be found in the Jacobite community and so, with some reluctance, James had agreed to the selection of an Italian woman. Otherwise, however, he was determined that no foreign habits or customs should contaminate his son's upbringing.

'The brave, lusty boy shall be dressed (as much as the climate will allow) in the English way,' he announced, 'for though I can't help his being born in Italy, yet as much as in me lies, he shall be English.' This was no ordinary baby, after all, but the rightful Prince of Wales.

The day after the baptism, the Pope celebrated Mass in the English church in Rome and, as word spread throughout Europe, thanksgiving services were held, bonfires were lit and more fireworks illuminated the night sky. For Jacobites everywhere, it was the best news that they had heard in years. At long last there was a new generation of royal Stuarts. The line was not going to dwindle away with a melancholy bachelor after all. Not only had James married, but he had provided himself with an heir, and suddenly the future seemed to hold all manner of exciting new possibilities.

In the nurseries the women fussed endlessly over the little Prince. His mother recovered rapidly from the birth and spent hours admiring her son while her ladies were kept busy conveying to the outside world the latest news of his progress. It was a gratifying task, for he was a large, healthy baby. There was only one minor setback when his nurse's milk did not seem to be agreeing with him, but that was soon remedied when she was replaced. Otherwise, Charles seemed bigger and more beautiful with each passing week and, as Lady Nithsdale said, 'every day [he] grows more charming'.

His adoring mother liked nothing better than to show him off to visitors, as two young gentlemen on the Grand Tour discovered. They were English, faithful subjects of George I and before they had left home their families had warned them against having anything to do with the claimant to the British throne. However, when they encountered James and Clementina strolling with their retinue through a Roman park, they found themselves being invited back to the Muti Palace that evening to attend a concert which the Queen had

24. *Charles as an infant*, a miniature possibly painted by L. Ramelli. (Reproduced by gracious permission of Her Majesty The Queen)

23. *Fireworks at St Peter's and the Vatican*, with the Castle Saint Angelo on the left. Detail of *Rome: La Girandola*, painted at a festival some years later, by Joseph Wright of Derby. (Walker Art Gallery, Liverpool)

organised. Unable to restrain their curiosity, they set off for the Street of the Holy Apostles in no little trepidation.

The concert proved excellent. The performers were the best musicians in the city, the audience consisted of all the leading members of high society and their hosts were graciousness itself, insisting that they stay on to dinner afterwards. The conversation over the meal was easy, even lighthearted. When James courteously drank a toast to English ladies in general, Clementina laughed and retorted in her deliciously accented English, 'I think, then, Sir, it would be but just that I drink to the cavaliers!'

After a good deal of such happy badinage, the Queen turned to the English guests and bade them accompany her to the nursery to see her son. At that, all their doubts came back with a guilty rush. As loyal supporters of George I they could hardly go and admire the offspring of the Stuart Pretender to his throne, but equally they could not decline without giving offence. They went.

Gazing at the baby Prince lying contentedly in his cradle, they were

forced to admit, 'He really is a fine, promising child', but they were considerably embarrassed by the behaviour of the British nurses. Delighted to have the opportunity of tormenting their fellow country-men, the wretched women leaned over the cradle, chattered, giggled and even insisted that the visitors should kiss the infant's hand. Covered in confusion, they hardly knew what to do, but they felt that they had to comply.

Clementina laughed heartily at their discomfiture and told them pointedly that they would not regret having made so early an acquaintance with her son. She obviously meant that one day they would be subjects of the Prince. It was difficult for them to think of an appropriate reply, but one of them had the wit to say 'that being hers, he [Charles] could not miss being good and happy'. At that, she took pity on them. The teasing ceased and they were allowed to rejoin the rest of the company.

If the Queen and her ladies were passionately devoted to the child, James III was even more concerned about his welfare. The responsibility

26. *Dr John Irwin*, physician to James III and his household, painted in 1739 by D. Dupra. (Scottish National Portrait Gallery)

of bringing up a Prince of Wales weighed heavily upon him, for he was determined that his son should be as perfect as possible in every way. Certainly a young infant had to be reared by women in his first months. The King realised that. However, in his opinion females were quarrelsome, unreliable and all too often lacking in sense, so he felt that he must keep a close watch on every aspect of life in the nursery.

Observing Mrs Hughes narrowly as she went about her business, he soon decided that she was not good enough to be the baby's principal attendant. She was kind and efficient, it was true, but she obviously came from a lowborn family. When Charles was old enough to be aware of his surroundings, who knew what undesirable habits he might pick up from her. James would tolerate her for the first year, he decided, and then he would replace her.

In the event, her departure was abrupt. The King discovered to his horror that Mrs Hughes had actually become involved in a plot to depose George I. She had no business playing politics. That in itself was bad enough, but what was so alarming about the whole affair was that she had agreed to smuggle Prince Charles over to England to take George's place. Such an escapade would have placed the baby in the most appalling danger. James summoned Mrs Hughes to the royal presence and dismissed her forthwith.

Turning over in his mind the question of a successor, he decided that she must have 'prudence, a reasonable knowledge of the world and a principle of attachment and submission to me, which may put her above private envies or factions'. He had the distinct impression that Clementina and her women were absurdly hostile to his perfectly natural interest in the nursery. The new nurse must realise from the start that she took orders from him and not from anyone else, not even the Queen.

Bearing in mind these criteria, he scrutinised various applicants and in the end, after due consideration, he selected Mrs Sheldon. The daughter of one of his father's equerries, she had been known to him from her earliest years. She seemed sensible, mature and respectful. She might even have a steadying influence on Clementina, whose deplorable impetuousness was making him increasingly uncomfortable.

Mrs Sheldon was accordingly installed in the nurseries and under her supervision the Prince continued to flourish. When he was nine months old, Lady Nithsdale was boasting that his first teeth were about to appear and at fifteen months he had four of them. It was high time he was weaned. This was an important and dangerous landmark in any eighteenth-century child's life. Following the continental and, indeed, the Scottish practice, his nurse's milk was abruptly withdrawn, rather than being gradually complemented with solids as was the way in England. One day, the nurse anointed her nipples with bitter aloes, Charles recoiled and 'after he had tasted it once, he would never look at the breast again'.

He came through the crisis unscathed, but it was not long before his

27. *Charles*, at the age of about four, by A. David. (In a private collection)

over-anxious father had found another cause for concern. Charles was 'not so forward on his feet as some children are at his age', Lady Nithsdale told a friend in Scotland, and when he was twenty months old she was still lamenting the fact that although he possessed seven fine teeth he was not yet walking. He was beginning to 'set his feet to the ground and stand against a place' but it was all rather worrying.

James III had no experience of small children. He had only had one younger sister and he had not paid any real attention to her childish accomplishments. Unable to gauge the significance of the situation, he was terrified that something might be amiss with Charles. Clementina and the nurses seemed annoyingly unconcerned and that made him worry even more. In a panic he sent for an eminent physician who examined the child and prescribed medicines.

When James passed on his instructions to Mrs Sheldon, she was furious. This was an affront to her personal dignity. How dared the King question her efficiency?

'As far as the advice sent by the famous doctor is concerned', she retorted frostily, 'I have the honour of informing you, Sire, that I do not consider that His Royal Highness is in any need of his remedies . . . I have no doubt that once this hot spell is over, he will walk very well . . . It is only the heat and his habit of leaning on his reins which hinders him.'

She was right, of course. The Prince learned to walk that winter and by spring he 'speaks everything and runs about from morning to night'. There was no need to be anxious about his health any more. In some respects they all settled back into their usual happy routine, but the atmosphere surrounding Charles was not as harmonious as it had once been.

His mother was becoming increasingly resentful of her husband's behaviour. She was a grown woman, the mother of his child, but he was still cold and reserved with her, treating her as if he were a heavy father rather than a loving partner. Volatile and quick-tempered, she was constantly quarrelling with him and the whole palace knew it. Their dispositions were so very different, Mr Hay told his wife, 'that though in the greatest trifles they are never of the same opinion, the one won't yield an inch to the other. The dread of being governed and the desire of governing: passion, youth engrafted by a little mean education will ever afford matter for supporting their differences, which must end in something very dismal. Their healths are equally ruined by it and it is impossible they can hold out so'.

After one particularly spectacular quarrel, Clementina flounced off to the baths at Lucca, saying that she was going for the sake of her health. Really, her departure was a desperate bid for James's attention, but he was far too dignified to go hurrying after her and she was reduced to plying him with gifts and artless little letters, telling him, 'I am trying to overcome my naughty temper so as to appear to you the best girl in the world'.

There was something disconcertingly childlike and innocent about Clementina, and if she was in one of her more contrite moods her husband found it easy enough to be kind to her. When he heard that her mother was dying, he did go to Lucca to comfort her and for a time they were friends once more but when they arrived back in Rome their arguments flared up again and before long they were spending much of their time together in huffy silence. Their only source of satisfaction seemed to be their son.

Tall for his age and well-made, the Prince was an enchanting child with dark red hair, large, brown eyes and a pretty, fair complexion. No one could remain morose for long in his exuberant company and when he was three Mr Hay noted admiringly that Charles was already 'a great musician and plays on his violin continually'. Moreover, he had a phenomenal amount of energy. 'No porter's child in the country has stronger legs and arms and he makes good use of them, for he is continually in motion . . . You may easily imagine what amusement he

gives to his Father and Mother, and indeed they have little other diversion.'

Happy at the centre of his own little world, the Prince seemed oblivious of the highly emotional atmosphere around him, but when he was four his settled routine was disturbed by a series of dramatic developments. On 6 March 1725 Clementina gave birth to a long awaited second child, another son, whom they named Henry Benedict Thomas Maria Francis Xavier. He was given the title Duke of York, and for the first time Charles had a rival for the attention of his admiring entourage.

Soon afterwards, the King decided that the time had come to remove him from the care of the nurses. James had become increasingly irritated at the sight of his firstborn running noisily about the Queen's apartments and even going off to visit the servants' quarters, where an indulgent and over-familiar audience awaited him. This was no way for a future king to behave. He needed stricter control and the authority of men, before the women ruined him entirely.

The choice of a governor was a very delicate matter and, of course, James never did anything hastily. After several false starts, he decided that the answer lay in his own household. Who could be more loyal and reliable than his faithful follower Mr James Murray? Mr Murray was well-educated, British and a Protestant. In the event of a restoration, he would be entirely acceptable to the British people, and

28. *The Baptism of Prince Henry*, in 1725, drawn by L. Sconzani.
(Bologna State Archives)

29. The Convent of
St Cecilia, where
Clementina retreated after
her quarrel with James III.
(Bibliotheca Hertziana,
Max-Planck Institut,
Rome)

the fact that the Prince was being taught by a Protestant would help to counterbalance the regrettable necessity of bringing up Charles in Rome, the centre of Catholicism. To safeguard the Prince's private, spiritual life, he would have a Catholic under-governor, a big, genial Irishman, Sir Thomas Sheridan. When he made the announcement, James also let it be known that he was giving Mr Murray a title. Henceforth he would be Earl of Dunbar. Charles was to quit the nurseries that very day and in future he would be accompanied at all times by the Earl or Sir Thomas.

When she heard the news, Clementina was appalled. To have her son taken from Mrs Sheldon and herself was a grievous blow, but the ultimate insult lay in the choice of Mr Murray, the man she had loathed for years. Personal feelings apart, it was unthinkable that her precious child should be committed to the care of a heretic. She raged, stormed and wept. James remained unmoved. He had made his decision and as far as he was concerned there was no more to be said.

At this worst of all times, a new crisis broke. Rumours swept round the court claiming that Mrs Hay had become the King's mistress. In her heart, Clementina probably did not believe it, but at this highly emotional moment it seemed to her that Mr Murray and Mr and Mrs Hay were the authors of all her troubles. As she and Mrs Sheldon whipped themselves up to new heights of indignation, the final blow fell. The King dismissed Mrs Sheldon. He had never liked her since her impudence over the affair of Charles's slowness in walking, and now he decreed that Prince Henry was to be cared for by the Protestant Lady Nithsdale.

Hysterical with rage, Clementina rushed into her husband's

chamber and threatened to leave him unless he sent away the hated Hays and the Earl of Dunbar. James stared at her in angry disbelief. This was the kind of behaviour which annoyed him most. No one was going to dictate to him. Coldly, he refused to reconsider, whereupon Clementina fled back to her own apartments. When she refused to come out, he wrote her a letter. He was convinced, he said, that the malicious lies of their enemies had 'imposed themselves on your youth and the follies of your sex'. That was hardly calculated to improve matters. First Mrs Sheldon departed in high dudgeon and then on 1 November Clementina summoned her coach, climbed in and drove to the Convent of St Cecilia. There she announced to the startled nuns that she had come to take refuge with them.

The nuns were deeply impressed by the tearful tale she had to tell and the Pope himself decided to intervene. The day after her sudden flight he sent one of his bishops to the Muti Palace to remonstrate with James. His Holiness could not tolerate the education of the princes as Protestants, he said, nor could he permit the King's liaison with Mrs Hay.

James was highly indignant. He advised the Bishop to mind his own business and he added that he could not believe that he was seriously being accused of adultery. The Bishop must have mistaken the Pope's meaning. If it were not that he realised that there must have been an error, the King concluded, the papal envoy would have run the risk of 'having to leave the house by the window instead of the staircase'. At that, the Bishop hastily took his departure.

Deeply mortified at his wife's behaviour, James decided to write her a stiff letter ordering her to come back at once. After all, he told her, he had been extraordinarily patient these past two years, 'when at times you scarcely wished to speak with me or look at me'. There was no question of him changing his mind about the tutors, of course. 'I will be master in my own affairs and in my own family', he wrote sternly, and he concluded, 'Return to reason, to duty, to yourself and to me, who await your submission with open arms.' Clementina did not reply.

At eight months, Prince Henry was too young to know what was happening, but Charles was nearly five and he must have been bewildered by the sudden disappearance of both his mother and his nurse. However, his father gave him no time to pine for Clementina. He carried his two sons off to Bologna and there he launched Charles into society. From their rented palace, they set off each day for balls, parties and concerts. The small Prince was seen dancing with girls his own age and also with adult ladies like the Countess Popoli. On his birthday a particularly grand party was given for him in the stately home of the Marescotti family, a thousand candles lighting up the lavishly decorated rooms. Everyone wore elaborate clothes and James III was gracious enough to take the lead in a suite of English dances. More balls followed throughout the carnival season and, by the time Lent came, Charles was established as the success of the social scene. The ladies in particular delighted in talking of his 'gallantry and

wit' and from then onwards, whenever he appeared in public, he was greeted with adulation and acclaim.

Back in Rome once more, life in the Muti Palace may have seemed dull by comparison, but there was little time for repining. According to his father's secretary, the Prince was improving 'daily in body and mind, to the admiration and joy of everybody'. He could read and speak English 'perfectly', although his spelling was erratic, and would remain so. He studied French and Italian too, and sporting activities were not neglected. He already possessed a stable of 'little horses' and every day he had riding lessons from the Chevalier Geraldi. His coordination was excellent and his skill at shooting was outstanding. 'I had seen him take a crossbow', an admiring relative reported, 'and kill birds on the roof and split a ball with a bolt ten times in succession'. Tennis, golf and shuttlecock were other regular diversions and he loved the hunting expeditions best of all.

There were also long talks with his father. The King discoursed about duty, responsibility, tolerance and humanity, and if the Prince did not fully understand his meaning, he was coming to a greater awareness of his own future role in life. Easier to comprehend were the stories of Sir Thomas Sheridan. The Irishman had a fund of fascinating tales about romantic knights, chivalrous combat and medieval adventure. His imagination already captured by the notion of these glorious warriors fighting for truth and justice, Charles was fired with the desire to act out a similar role himself.

Meanwhile, his father strove to put his own private life to rights, urged on by the Jacobites who feared that Britain would never accept as king one who could not even keep his wife in order. The need for a reconciliation with Clementina became all the more urgent when James learned that George I was dying. At that point, the Pope took a hand. He indicated to Clementina that she might be refused the sacraments if she did not keep her marriage vows by living with her husband. That threat succeeded where all others had failed. While James was away in north-west France after George's death, consulting friends about what he should do next, the Queen suddenly emerged from her convent, arriving at the family's summer residence in Bologna for a tearful reunion with her sons. Shortly afterwards James, abandoning all thought of a new British invasion, joined them.

31. *Clementina kneeling in prayer*, engraved in 1737 from a painting by A. Masucci. (Scottish National Portrait Gallery)

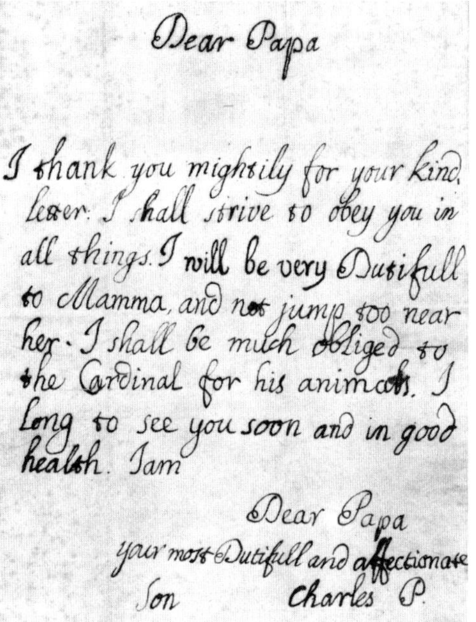

32. Letter from Charles, aged about eight, promising to behave in his mother's company. (Windsor Castle, Royal Library, © 1987. Reproduced by gracious permission of Her Majesty The Queen)

They were all mightily relieved to see Clementina and recollections of her previous tiresome behaviour were swept away by their surprise at the change in her. The pretty, pouting little girl had gone forever. In her place was a thin, frail, beautiful woman whose whole being seemed to burn with a fierce spiritual energy. She was genuinely moved to see her sons again, but for the most part her mind was fixed on her religious observances. She prayed for hours on end, visited innumerable convents to view holy relics and had endless discussions with the nuns. She did not eat with the rest of the family. While James and the Princes dined in state at the Muti Palace she sat at her own little table alongside, picking at the frugal repast set before her according to her own careful instructions.

The King and his sons were bewildered. 'She leads a most singular life', James told Mr Hay. 'She takes no manner of amusement, not even taking the air, and when she is not at church or at table, is locked up in her room, but sees no mortal but her maids . . . I am very little with her. I let her do what she will.' She slept with him, of course, but it seemed unlikely that anyone who fasted so stringently could bear children and indeed, although she had two false pregnancies, there were to be no more babies.

Eventually, the family grew accustomed to her strange, sweet, other-worldly ways and they all felt the need to cherish and protect her. Even the boisterous Charles promised solemnly, 'I will be very dutiful to Mama and not jump too near her'. She seemed happy in her own peculiar way and when a charismatic friar arrived in Rome preaching poverty and the care of the underprivileged, she found new fulfilment nursing the destitute, although she herself was suffering

33. *A Fete in the Piazza Navona, Rome*, in 1729, by G. P. Panini. James and his sons attended the celebrations in honour of the birth of the French Dauphin.
(National Gallery of Ireland)

33(*a*) Detail of 33, showing James with Charles and Henry.

wretchedly from asthma. Soon, the people of Rome were praising her as a saint.

More than ever now, the King's thoughts were concentrated on his children. Henry was his favourite. Charles's overpowering energy was wearing and the process of transforming him into the perfect prince was sometimes more of a trial than a pleasure. His younger brother was more like James in personality: serious, introspective and generally well-behaved. 'I really am in love with the little Duke', the King confided to a friend, 'for he is the finest child that can be seen.'

Both boys had fierce tempers, it was true, but James dealt with that in his own way. When Henry had a tantrum his father ceremoniously withdrew his Orders of the Thistle and the Garter, and when Charles quarrelled with his tutor and threatened to kill him he was locked in his room. Some of the courtiers felt that the King set unreasonably high standards of behaviour for his sons, but when Mr Hay ventured to caution him against being too harsh with Charles, James merely replied wearily, 'There is no question of crushing the Prince's spirit and no danger of its being crushed, for he is mightily thoughtless and takes nothing much to heart'.

His immediate solution for Charles was to send him off on a military campaign. The boy was thirteen now, 'he has good health and cannot begin too soon to learn his métier'. Accompanied by his two tutors and using the pseudonym the Chevalier de St George, Charles travelled to Gaeta, which his relative the Duke of Liria was besieging on behalf of the Spanish. The Prince was thrilled and he enjoyed every moment of the expedition: the noise of the cannonballs exploding really quite close to him, the bustle and action of the military camp and the admiring comradeship of the soldiers. When the town fell, Charles sailed to Naples where he stayed for a month, sharing in the congratulatory atmosphere and being treated as though he himself were a hero. Even his father's adversaries were impressed. 'Everybody says that he will be in time a far more dangerous enemy to the present establishment of the government of England than ever his father did', a Hanoverian spy remarked.

When he set off for home, the Prince rode in procession with a guard of fifty soldiers, proudly taking with him two magnificent horses presented to him by the King of Spain. If he hoped that his father would be impressed with him at last, he was sadly disappointed.

35. *Henry*, also with Garter sash, painted that same year by A. David. (Scottish National Portrait Gallery)

36. *Clementina Sobieska lying in state*, engraved from a picture by G. P. Panini. (Scottish National Portrait Gallery)

37. Memorial to Clementina in St Peter's, Rome. (Photograph, Vatican Museums)

Instead of welcoming him back as a valiant hero, the King launched into a tirade about Charles's failure to write to him more than twice. Henry had not heard from him at all, he said, and he reminded him, as he had so often done before, of his 'too natural aversion to all application and constraint'.

His father's irritability was understandable, for the King and the entire household were deeply concerned about Clementina's health. She had become dreadfully emaciated and although she was only thirty-two her doctors were predicting that she would not recover from this latest illness. She lingered on for a few months more but she really had worn herself out and on 12 January 1735 she received the last rites. Her family were distraught.

'She is perfectly in her senses', the King reported, 'and dies with a tranquillity, a piety and a peace which is, with reason, a great comfort to me in my present situation', but when the end came six days later he nearly fainted, and the princes were 'almost sick with weeping and want of sleep'. No matter how they might have quarrelled in the past, James, Clementina and their sons had remained a close family, confiding in each other and trusting each other more than they did any outsiders. After all, they shared the unique bond of being royal, and no matter how well-disposed they might be to their advisers and their courtiers, there remained a very real gulf between monarch and subjects.

38. *Charles*, aged about
fourteen, by Giles Hussey,
an Irish artist at James III's
court in Rome.
(The Duke of Atholl, at
Blair Castle: photograph,
Scotland's Story)

39. Drawing done by
Charles as a child,
presumably copied from a
painting or engraving.
(In a Scottish private
collection)

On the Pope's personal orders, Clementina was given a magnificent funeral. After lying in state in the Church of the Holy Apostles, her body was carried to St Peter's, arrayed in a velvet and ermine cloak, a gold crown on her head and an ivory sceptre in her hand. James and the princes, wearing black velvet, watched from the palace windows as the solemn procession wound its way down the Street of the Holy Apostles, and then they attended the Requiem Mass. The service over, Clementina was buried in the crypt of St Peter's, her royal robes replaced by the plain black and white garments of a Dominican nun. Her husband and her sons spent the rest of the day in prayer.

If James had been morose before, he sank even deeper into depression now and 'Old Mr Melancholy', the nickname given to him by the Hanoverians, was cruelly apt. Charles remained a perpetual source of worry, too. 'He continues wonderfully thoughtless for his age', his father complained. The boy seemed 'very innocent and backward in some respects' and instead of applying himself to his studies he wasted his time on 'little childish amusements'. In yet another attempt to make a man of him, he sent him off on a tour of the Italian cities, and Charles proved a great success, delighting everyone he met with his graciousness, his charm and his kindness to old people.

He had almost reached his full height of five feet ten inches, and he looked even taller because of his slender build. In features, as in

40. *The Muti Palace,
decorated for the coronation of
Pope Benedict XIV in 1740,
by G. P. Panini.*
(Hamilton Collection at
Lennoxlove)

40(*a*) Detail of 41, showing
Charles and Henry in
conversation behind their
father.

disposition, he was very like his mother. He had a long, oval face,
large, dark brown eyes, a neat, aquiline nose and a generous mouth.
His hair was dark red and until he was sixteen he wore it long. His
devoted valet rolled it up in curl papers each night so that it would
hang to his waist in an elegant bunch of ringlets.

Back in Rome once more, he remained the centre of attention. He
was the guest of honour at all the balls and parties, usually appearing
in satins and jewels but sometimes wearing the complete set of
highland dress sent to him from Scotland by the Duke of Perth.

Wherever he went the ladies were greatly taken with him, and if he seemed indifferent to them that merely served to make them more attentive.

His mind was on other matters. At one ball he had been heard to remark, 'Had I soldiers I would not be here now, but wherever I could serve my friends'. The King might believe him to be idle and thoughtless, but Sir Thomas Sheridan's romantic tales and his own desperate desire to win his father's approval had combined to give him one fierce, single-minded ambition. He would win back Britain for the King. Until then, all other activities would take a lesser place.

The public appearances at social events came as second nature now. He could be gracious and pleasant without even having to think about it. The hours spent hunting and shooting had a much more serious purpose. They were training for the battlefield. So too were the long, barefoot country walks. Indoors, he pored over military manuals, plans of fortifications and model forts. The only recreation he permitted himself was an hour or two spent playing the cello in the evening. Otherwise, his day was full, for he was always aware of the fact that, sooner or later, the summons would come. He would be asked to lead an invasion of Britain, and he must be fully prepared.

42. *Charles*, aged eighteen, by L. G. Blanchet. (Reproduced by gracious permission of Her Majesty The Queen)

3

FRANCE

IN THE late autumn of 1743, when the Prince was twenty-two, the message came at last. Louis XV wanted him to go to Paris. France and Britain were at war, the French had recently suffered a serious defeat at Dettingen and now they were seeking revenge. They would invade England, depose George II and proclaim James III as King instead. There was no point in expecting him to go in person but they would take his son along, so that the British Jacobites would help them. Charles would then govern the country as Regent for his father.

The Prince received the news with delight. After all the years of preparation, his time had finally come. The eyes of the world were upon him and he would show everyone that the Stuart family was not doomed to perpetual exile. The prospect of an expedition was enthralling and even James was excited. He would worry dreadfully about Charles's safety, of course, but as he himself remarked, 'It is now or never'. On 23 December 1743 he signed a document appointing his son to be 'sole Regent of our kingdoms of England, Scotland and Ireland' and then he and the Prince began to make their plans.

Everything had to be done in the strictest secrecy: George II must on no account find out what was going on. In any event, it was illegal for the Prince to enter France at all. Some years before, the French had signed an international treaty promising not to harbour any member of the royal Stuart family. Charles would have to go in disguise and if he were discovered the French would deny all knowledge of him. The Prince's governor, the Earl of Dunbar, was taken into his confidence, but otherwise not even Prince Henry knew what was going on. The Muti Palace was always full of spies and the boy might give something away by his very attitude if not by what he said. He was only eighteen and he had still to learn how to dissemble convincingly.

As soon as New Year was past, Charles announced that he was taking Henry on a boar hunting trip to Cisterna. On 9 January 1744, before dawn, he bade his father farewell, declaring fervently, 'I go, Sire, in search of three crowns, which I doubt not to have the honour and happiness of laying at Your Majesty's feet. If I fail in the attempt, your next sight of me shall be in my coffin!'

His father flinched. 'Heaven forbid that all the crowns in the world should rob me of my son!' he exclaimed, and he embraced him tenderly, murmuring 'Be careful of yourself, my dear Prince, for my sake and, I hope, for the sake of millions'.

There was no time for any further conversation. Henry and the others were waiting. A moment later, they were riding along the Street of the Holy Apostles, past the quiet houses and palaces of the early Roman morning and away to the countryside beyond.

42. *Louis XV*, by
L. M. Van Loo.
(Versailles: photograph,
Clichés des Musées
Nationaux, Paris)

43. *George II*, on the eve of the Jacobite rising, painted in 1744 by Thomas Hudson. (National Portrait Gallery, London)

They had not gone very far when Henry was alarmed to hear a loud crash and a muffled shout. Turning to investigate, he found that the Earl of Dunbar had somehow contrived to fall into a ditch. They pulled him out, set him on his feet, brushed him down and enquired anxiously if he was all right. He was winded, but apparently unharmed. Reassured, Henry looked round for his brother, but the Prince was nowhere to be seen. He must have ridden on ahead. The others set off to follow, but they did not catch up with him, and an hour or two later one of his grooms came riding back to say that he had sprained his ankle. It was nothing serious, but he would rest for a while at Frascati. Not for several days would Henry discover the true course of events.

In fact, the Prince, disguised as a courier in an old cloak, was spurring onwards towards Pisa. He had one groom with him, and he

44. *James III* in about 1741,
by or after F. Ponzone.
(National Portrait Gallery,
London)

was joined on the way by Sir Thomas Sheridan's nephew Michael, and
by Colonel John O'Sullivan, an amiable, talkative Irishman who had
been serving with the French army. They would travel together. It was
far too dangerous to go all the way to France by sea, for the British fleet
was patrolling the Mediterranean. Instead, they would make their way
round the coast of the Gulf of Genoa.

A few miles north of Pisa, they boarded a Maltese boat sailing to
Genoa. From there they rode to Savona, to embark on a Catalan
fellucca bound for Antibes. At first the Prince announced himself as
Don Biagio, a Spanish officer, then he became 'Mr Graham', a Scottish
traveller. Sailing boldly through the middle of the British fleet, they
finally arrived in France on 23 January. They were at once taken into
quarantine, and the Prince was informed that he was to stay in Antibes
until Louis XV sent for him.

That did not please him at all. There must be some mistake, he
protested. Louis could not possibly want him to kick his heels in a little
seaside town on the fringes of France after his urgent journey from
Rome. He would ride on. A local official tried to remonstrate with him,
but it was no use. His mind was made up. The official then offered to
lend him his chaise, saying that the Prince could never endure the
fatigue of riding all the way to Paris. The Prince replied that he
intended doing precisely that. His luggage could go in the chaise. So
saying, he mounted a post horse and galloped off.

45. Silver gilt travelling canteen of cutlery, made in Edinburgh for the Prince in 1740–1 and sent to him, probably as a present for his 21st birthday. He took it with him to Scotland and it eventually fell into Cumberland's hands after Culloden.
(National Museums of Scotland)

Apart from a brief rest at Lyons, he set a tremendous pace, covering the distance to the capital in less than a fortnight. Even he was forced to admit that he was 'a little fatigued' when he got there, but he soon recovered and joked apologetically about wearing out his companions. 'If I had been to go much further', he said, 'I should have been obliged to get them tied behind the chaise with my portmanteau, for they were quite exhausted.' None of that mattered now, though. They had arrived, they were within a few miles of 'my Uncle Louis' and at any moment the Prince expected to receive a summons to the royal presence.

The French kept warning him that he must not reveal his true identity until their King gave him permission, so he had to find unobtrusive lodgings where no one would suspect who he really was. There were various Jacobites in Paris and he went to stay with Lord Sempill and William MacGregor of Balhaldy, two Scotsmen acting as his father's agents. They were overjoyed to see him and although they knew that his expedition was bound for London, they lost no time in praising the loyalty and enthusiasm of their own fellow-countrymen.

The Scots had long been groaning under Hanoverian rule, they claimed, and the highlanders in particular were waiting eagerly for the Prince to come and lead them into battle.

Amidst a whirl of new impressions, Charles passed that first week. Lord Sempill had been given 10,000 livres by the French government for the Prince's personal use. The money was very necessary, of course, but what he really wanted was a summons to an audience with Louis XV. He waited confidently, albeit with growing impatience, but no invitation came. Instead, the French King sent him a message instructing him to travel to Gravelines, a little Channel port twelve miles west of Dunkirk. He would travel incognito, needless to say, and there could be no meeting with Louis before he went.

Charles was puzzled, and more than a little annoyed, but he had to obey his instructions. Calling himself 'the Chevalier Douglas' and taking Balhaldy with him to act as his secretary, he rode north. He rented modest lodgings in Gravelines and entertained himself for hours on end by watching the French fleet assembling in the Channel. The preparations were impressive 10,000 men were to sail in transport

46. The canteen's thirty-one pieces include a nutmeg grater, a corkscrew and a cruet as well as knives, forks and spoons. They fit into two wine beakers, within an outer case.
(National Museums of Scotland)

vessels and the expedition was to be led by the renowned Field Marshal Saxe. The Prince himself would be the nominal commander, of course.

Absorbed in all that was going on around him, he ignored rumours that Saxe wanted no part in this invasion and that a number of government ministers shared his view that the war in Flanders was far more important. Charles took the attitude that Saxe's personal foibles were of no significance. Louis had ordered the invasion, and that alone mattered.

By the beginning of March, everything was ready. The transport vessels began to set sail and a small French fleet went ahead to make sure that the way was clear. It was not. Spies had long since warned George II of what was happening and the British navy was lying in wait in the Strait of Dover.

Before any encounter could take place, however, a tremendous storm blew up, smashing the protective French vessels and tearing at those transport ships which had already set out. The Prince and Saxe managed to reach safety, but when morning came, dreadful damage was revealed. Several ships had been lost with everyone aboard,

eleven vessels had run aground and even those which had not left harbour were badly battered.

Word went swiftly back to Paris. The French ministers held urgent meetings and just a week after the disastrous storm it fell to Field Marshal Saxe to break the news to the Prince. There would be no invasion of Britain that year.

Charles received his message with utter disbelief. Although he had witnessed the havoc wrought by the storm he had not for one minute imagined that the expedition would be cancelled. He had been preparing himself for years for this moment: it could not possibly be snatched away now. The Prince was like his mother. When he set his heart on something, he could not be deflected. Warnings, advice, obstacles and disappointments made no difference. He was determined that he would have his own way and he pursued his ambitions with a pertinacity which surprised and sometimes horrified even his greatest friends.

He now declared that if no one else would go, he would set sail himself. It was no use travelling to London without an army. Instead, he would make for Scotland. All the faithful highlanders would rise in

48. Engraving commemorating the unsuccessful naval expedition of March 1744. The Prince is supported by the figures of Hope and Time, while the storm rages in the background, wrecking the French fleet. (Scottish National Portrait Gallery)

49. *George, 10th Earl Marischal*, James III's trusted adviser, by P. Parrocel.
(Scottish National Portrait Gallery)

his favour and, he told Lord Sempill, 'I would rather die at the head of these brave men than languish in exile and dependence.' The thought of returning ignominiously to Rome was too terrible to contemplate.

The Jacobites in Paris were alarmed when they learned of his intentions and the Earl Marischal, one of his father's most trusted advisers, set off at once for Gravelines to restrain him. As soon as he saw the Earl, Charles suggested that the pair of them should hire a boat and set out for Scotland right away. Appalled, the Earl told him that he must not consider such a rash course of action. It was out of the question. He would not only risk his own life but he would jeopardise the entire Stuart cause.

The Prince saw the sense of that and he was forced to admit that the Earl was right. However, he could not bear to leave Gravelines and so he stayed on, hoping against hope that the French might change their minds. He was still living incognito, and his way of life afforded him some amusement as well as a good deal of frustration.

'The situation I am in is very particular,' he told his father in a letter dated 3 April, 'for nobody knows where I am or what has become of me, so that I am entirely buried as to the public and can't but say that it is a very great constraint upon me, for I am obliged very often not to stir out of my room for fear of somebody knowing my face. I very often think that you would laugh very heartily if you saw me going about with a single servant, buying fish and other things and squabbling for a penny more or less.'

It was a far cry from the balls, the operas and the flattery of the courtiers in Rome, but his resolve remained unshaken. 'I hope Your Majesty will be thoroughly persuaded', he went on, 'that no constraint or trouble whatsoever of mind or body will ever stop me in going on with my duty, in doing anything that I think can tend to your service and glory.'

Far away in Rome, James III certainly did not feel like smiling when he heard of his son's situation. 'The promises of France are not to be reconciled with her negligent and indifferent behaviour towards the Prince', he told Lord Sempill angrily, and his greatest worry was that Charles in his frustration would concoct some foolhardy plan. Presumably he had heard all about the Prince's desire to go to Scotland, for he wrote urging him to 'avoid precipitate and dangerous measures, some rash or ill-conceived project which would end in your ruin and in that of all those who would join with you in it'.

In the end it was not his father's advice which made the Prince quit the coast, but a new series of rumours. Reports from Paris indicated that Louis XV was planning to go to Flanders in person and it was hinted that he might even consider taking Charles with him. This was not what the Prince had in mind, but it would give him access to the French King and while they were with the army together he could surely convince Louis of the necessity of the British expedition.

Full of optimism, he set off for the capital. There the Earl Marischal had already vetoed the plan, explaining to the French authorities that it would prejudice Charles's interests completely if he were seen fighting on the French side against British soldiers on the continent. That would antagonise all his supporters in England. In spite of this, the Prince continued for months to cherish hopes of accompanying Louis and his thoughts of the future were divided between his long-term aims and this more immediate opportunity for military action.

While he waited to see what would happen, he established himself in a pleasant little house near Montmartre and decided to send to Rome for Sir Thomas Sheridan. Balhaldy was not an adequate

50. *Louis XV hunting in the forest of Compiègne*: design for a tapestry at Fontainebleau, by J. B. Oudry. (Fontainebleau: photograph, Giraudon)

secretary: he needed someone he could really trust, and his old under-governor was completely loyal to him. Sir Thomas was elderly and in failing health; however, he complied gladly with his beloved Prince's summons. 'Poor man, he will not hold out long', said a friend, but by taking the journey in easy stages he finally arrived in Paris for a joyful reunion with Charles. He wrote to tell James all about the pretty little house, the agreeable air and, most of all, about the Prince himself.

'I found him in very good health', he reported, 'and he seemed to me both taller and broader than when I saw him last. He is certainly increased in bulk; but for his height . . .', that was more puzzling. Surely he had been fully grown for some time now, and yet he seemed taller. 'When I seemed surprised at it', Sir Thomas continued, 'he let me into the secret. He showed me the heels of his shoes which he wears now of the usual size, whereas before he wore them remarkably lower than other people. In fine, he has altogether a much more manly air than he had when he began his travels.'

The Prince was just as pleased to see him, although Sir Thomas was really past carrying out the tasks required of him. Charles could not bear to see him labouring painfully over the business of translating his confidential letters into code and so, for a time, he took over that tedious duty himself. It was a nuisance, but Sir Thomas served him well in another capacity for he was his only really trustworthy companion.

Throughout that slow summer the Prince waited in vain for any encouragement from the French Court. Louis XV was well disposed towards him, he felt sure, but the government ministers were devious, elusive and full of empty promises. He was becoming increasingly disillusioned with them and so it was with all the more interest that he greeted a new visitor from an entirely different quarter.

In August, there arrived in Paris John Murray of Broughton. The son of an ardent Jacobite, and a lawyer by training, he had been acting as James III's agent in Scotland. In recent months the Jacobites there had become increasingly bewildered about what was going on. They had heard reports of the Prince's arrival in Paris, they had listened to rumours about an invasion of Britain and they had waited anxiously for something to happen. Instead, there had been a long and puzzling silence, with Balhaldy making no attempt to keep them informed about the cancellation of the expedition. When they could bear it no longer, they decided to send Murray to Paris to see for himself what was really being done.

A series of secret meetings with Charles was arranged at the Great Stables at the Tuileries, where Murray explained himself. During his conversations with the Prince, he warned him that the number of Jacobite supporters in Scotland was far smaller than Sempill and Balhaldy had alleged. Many Scots were perfectly content with Hanoverian rule and the prosperity it had brought them, he said. As for the committed Jacobites, most of the clan chiefs were convinced that this was not a suitable time for a rising. They were more worried that the Prince would come than afraid that he would not.

Charles listened intently to all that Murray had to tell him, but instead of being disappointed at the Scottish response, his enthusiasm for the campaign increased visibly. He announced with 'great keenness' that he was 'determined to come the following summer, though with a single footman'. In dismay, Murray exclaimed that such a scheme would never succeed. The Prince must have troops if he were to go north. At this, Charles repeated what he had just said, 'with still greater energy', and throughout the ensuing discussions he declared himself 'unalterably fixed in his resolution to make an attempt'. The idea had been in his mind ever since Gravelines and now this direct contact with Scotland made it no longer seem a vague notion but an exciting reality. He could not set out yet, of course, for there were preparations to be made, and he had no money. In fact, he was every day running deeper into debt. Somehow, he had to put his finances on a sounder basis and then he could begin to plan in earnest.

Towards the end of the year, he let it be known that he was longing to go back to Italy. He could not leave, of course, without satisfying his creditors. When they heard that, the French ministers were so anxious to be rid of his embarrassing presence that they offered not only to pay all his debts but to increase his pension to 5000 livres a month. They even agreed that he could meet some of his own relatives before he left.

That was gratifying news indeed. For so long now his alias had constrained him to see only a very limited circle of exiled Jacobites, but now a whole new world opened up before him. His mother's elder sister, the flippant, frivolous Charlotte, had married the Duke of

51. View of Versailles. (Photograph, Dr David Breeze)

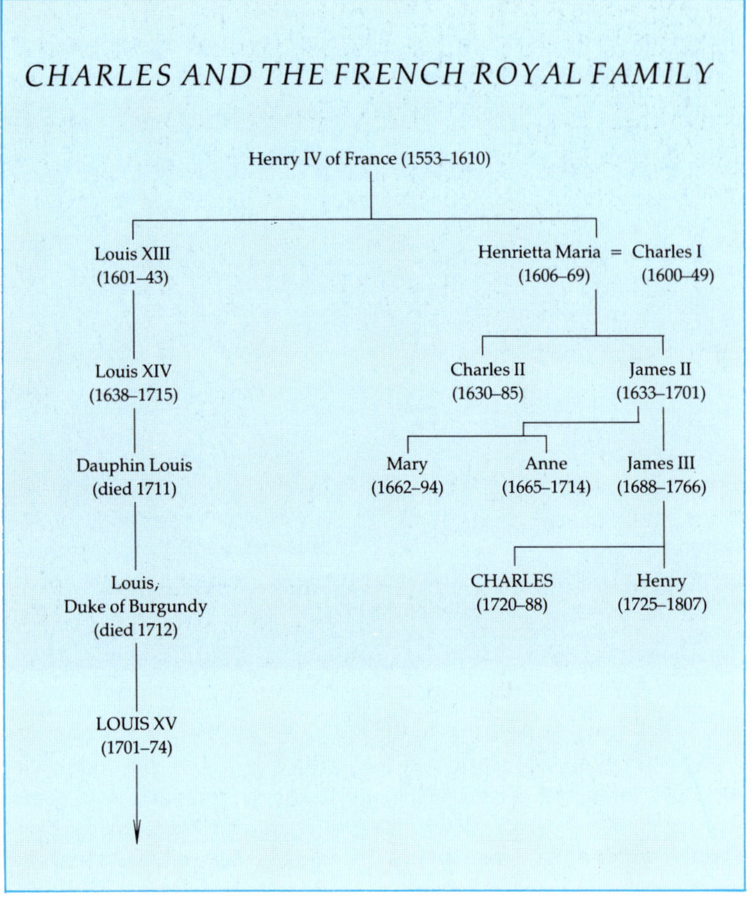

Bouillon. She herself was dead, but the Duke was Grand Chamberlain of France and an intimate friend of Louis XV. An influential and powerful man, he was a contact well worth cultivating. He also had two children, Charles's cousins. Louise, just nineteen, had recently married and she was pregnant. Godfrey Charles, her younger brother, was a pleasant lad of sixteen.

James III had always kept up with the Bouillon family, even after Clementina's death. Certainly he had done no more than exchange seasonal greetings with them, and news of family births, deaths and marriages, but the Duke now invited Charles to supper and they immediately took to one another. The young people were friendly and high-spirited, the Duke was kindness itself and within days they were all going out together to parties, concerts and operas.

The balls at court were huge affairs, attended by several thousand people at a time, and the dancers wore masks. It was perfectly possible for Charles to mingle unrecognised with the crowd and when anyone spoke to him he said that he was a German baron. In spite of warnings that the King was displeased with his public outings he persisted in going to Versailles and at one masked ball there he sat down

deliberately near the Queen herself. Taken with the appearance of the slender, elegant young gentleman, she asked who he was. A quick-thinking lady-in-waiting hastily replied, 'My brother', and Her Majesty did not discover the true identity of the mysterious guest until some days later.

Much as he might enjoy these lighthearted occasions with their spice of danger, the Prince had not forgotten his true reason for being in Paris. Indeed, his repeated visits to Versailles were made in the hope

52. *Marie Leszczynska*, Louis XV's Polish Queen, by J. M. Nattier. (Versailles: photograph, Clichés des Musées Nationaux, Paris)

that he could somehow introduce himself to the King. When that proved impossible, he concentrated on persuading his uncle to speak to Louis on his behalf and there is every indication that the Duke did so. From then onwards, Charles appeared to have received indirect encouragement in his Scottish plans. After all, a diversion in the north was always a good idea and if Charles went to Scotland, apparently on his own initiative, the French had nothing to lose. They would simply disclaim all knowledge of him if the scheme failed.

In the early weeks of 1745 the Prince was dividing his time between Fitzjames, the country residence of a relative, and the capital itself. To all appearances he was merely hunting, riding and enjoying himself. In reality, he was beginning the preparations for his daring enterprise. Reports from Scotland indicated that the highlanders lacked weapons. After the rising in 1715 the government had forbidden them to carry arms. Charles therefore persuaded his banker to lend him 180,000 livres and with this sum he set about purchasing broadswords and muskets.

He also augmented his retinue by taking on as master of his household Colonel John O'Sullivan, one of the Irishmen who had accompanied him on his journey to France. O'Sullivan's experience of guerrilla warfare in Italy would be useful for Scotland. At first, the Colonel was not allowed to know why he had really been employed, but he grew suspicious when Sir Thomas kept asking him about ships and suppliers of arms and he was finally taken into their confidence. He then set about helping with the purchase of the weapons and he bought a number of personal items for the Prince: several cases of pistols, a travelling chest for clothes, a bed and a set of plate.

Events were moving swiftly now and there remained only the problem of transport. Borrow as he might, the Prince could not afford to purchase a vessel to take him to Scotland and so he decided to hire one instead. Each year the French granted official licences to captains

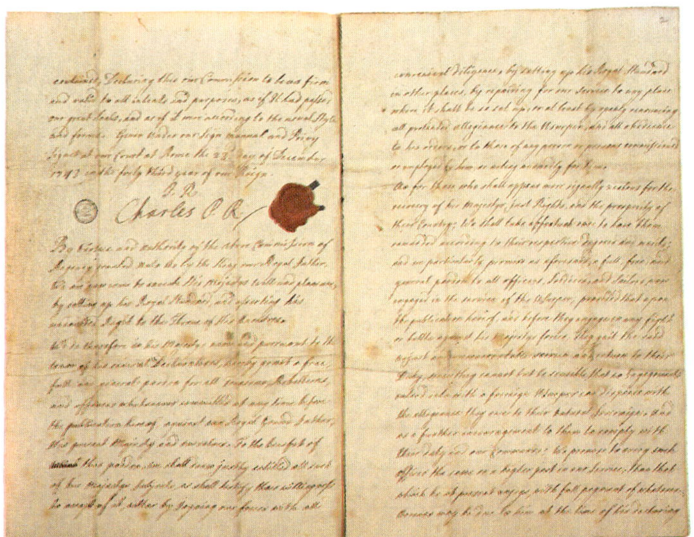

53. Proclamation by Charles to the people of Great Britain, pardoning those who had opposed his grandfather James II. Issued at Paris on 16 May 1745.
(National Library of Scotland)

willing to sail into British waters as privateers. This was a useful way of harassing the enemy and the captains were allowed to keep whatever prizes they took. Walter Rutledge, a merchant of Dunkirk, had obtained just such a licence for his large old ship, the *Elisabeth* and he was willing to hire it to the Prince.

Rutledge's piratical activities would provide the ideal cover. Charles also needed a smaller, faster vessel in which to travel himself and this was provided by Antoine Walsh, a former French naval officer of Irish descent. He had made a fortune in the slave trade and his light frigate the *Du Teillay* was ideally suited for the purpose. Various official licences and documents were needed, of course, but the French government granted them, presumably knowing perfectly well for what they were really wanted.

In May, the French won a notable victory over the British at Fontenoy and Charles knew that the way ahead was clear. Almost all Britain's troops were on the continent, their morale was low after their crushing defeat and Scotland had been left virtually undefended. It was time to go.

Throughout all the weeks of careful planning, Charles had been at pains to keep his activities secret, not only from the British but from his own father. He was convinced that if he were to ask James for permission to sail to Scotland, the King would refuse. However, the time had come when he could no longer conceal his intentions and so he sat down to compose a letter explaining his motives.

Conversations with friends from Scotland, he wrote, had convinced him that if he did not mount an invasion that year, the Jacobites would rise anyway, in the belief that 'the worst that could happen to them was to die in the field which was preferable to living any longer in misery and oppression'. He genuinely believed that he was going to deliver the Scots from a cruel and tyrannical ruler. The responsibility for the scheme was his alone, he declared, and he was confident that his father would forgive him. After all, James had taken part in just such an expedition some thirty years before.

The letter written, he penned a briefer one to Louis XV in a tone which was both courteous and reproachful. Since His Majesty had failed to give him the help he had so often requested, he said, he had decided to act on his own. The scheme he had devised would be infallible if he received the minimum of assistance. Since it would, as he put it, 'allow me to play a role worthy of my birth', he hoped that Louis and his ministers might now supply him with a measure of aid.

Fearing that he might still be ordered to stay where he was, he made sure that neither of these letters would arrive before his departure by sending them by the most circuitous routes possible. He then disguised himself as the Chevalier Douglas, a student of the Scots College in Paris, and set off for Nantes where Walsh and the others were waiting. For some reason, Walsh felt that the student garb was not a good idea and instead he fitted the Prince out as an Irish priest. In plain black clothes he would be much less recognisable, for his true identity was to be kept even from the men of the *Du Teillay*.

Scattered throughout the town were the leading conspirators, an unlikely collection of Irish and Scots, most of them well past their first youth. Sir Thomas Sheridan was determined not to be left behind, in spite of his infirmities. Colonel O'Sullivan would pose as the Prince's father. William, Marquis of Tullibardine, middle-aged and crippled with rheumatism, was the rightful Duke of Atholl, having lost his title to his brother after his participation in the '15.

Of the rest, Sir John MacDonald, an elderly, drunken cavalry officer did at least have some military experience, but the other three did not. Parson Kelly was an Irish priest, Francis Strickland had been Prince Henry's tutor until James III dismissed him in disgrace and Aeneas Macdonald, a banker, did not really want to go at all. He had been travelling to Scotland anyway and he was persuaded to go with the Prince against his better judgment. Accompanying him was his clerk; the Prince had a chaplain, valet and groom, and there were several domestic servants.

Next morning, they sailed down the Loire to St Nazaire, where the *Du Teillay* rode at anchor. To their annoyance, contrary winds and a series of bureaucratic delays forced them to wait at Belle Isle for the *Elisabeth*, but she appeared at last, carrying men and the supplies purchased by the Prince: 1500 muskets, 1800 broadswords, twenty small field guns and a good quantity of powder, ball, flints, dirks and brandy. The 700 men on board included a company of sixty officers and cadets of the French navy: further evidence of the government's complicity in the scheme. The Prince was particularly pleased to see them. They might be disappointingly few in number, but they would 'make a show, having a pretty uniform'.

On 5 July, they set sail. The seas were calm and the first part of the voyage passed uneventfully, but on 9 July they suddenly saw before them the *Lyon*, a large British naval vessel travelling from Spithead to join a squadron in the Bay of Biscay. Because the *Elisabeth* was so much slower, her French captain was forced to engage the *Lyon* in battle, but

Walsh was horrified at the prospect. He knew the identity of his precious passenger and he was conscious of the fact that his frigate was made for speed, not warfare. If the worst came to the worst, he would shelter behind the larger ship.

At about five o'clock that afternoon, battle was joined. The *Elisabeth* boldly fired a broadside at the *Lyon*, whereupon the *Lyon* fired back with damaging accuracy. Aiming for her enemy's mizzen mast, the *Elisabeth* then managed to bring down considerable quantities of the *Lyon*'s rigging, suffering serious casualties herself as she did so. Aboard the *Du Teillay*, the Prince was desperate to go to her aid but Walsh would not allow it. When Charles argued, he threatened to send him below. He might be the King's son, but aboard this ship he must accept the authority of the captain like everyone else. They remained where they were, watching the action avidly and, almost in spite of themselves, admiring the superior skill of the British.

By nightfall, however, the *Lyon* had suffered such serious damage and had sustained so many casualties that she began to move away. Forty-five of her sailors had been killed and over 100 were injured. On the *Elisabeth* the situation was even worse. The French captain and his brother both lay dead, with fifty-seven of his men, and there were a further 167 casualties. They were in no condition to pursue the enemy vessel, and in any event there was the danger that they might encounter further British naval ships. After a hurried council of war, they agreed that the *Elisabeth* would limp back to France. The *Du Teillay* thereupon doused all her lights except the small, shaded one above the compass, and set sail in the opposite direction. She would go on to Scotland alone.

56. *A Naval Engagement* showing the *Lyon* and the *Elisabeth* joining battle, with the *Du Teillay* visible in the background. Painted soon after the event, by P. Monamy. (In a private collection)

4

THE GLORIOUS ENTERPRISE

ON 22 July 1745* the travellers aboard the *Du Teillay* had their first sight of Scotland. Through mist and driving rain they could see land ahead of them. It was Bernera, a small island at the southern tip of the Outer Hebrides. As they all crowded to the side to watch the island take shape before them, the Marquis of Tullibardine pointed to the sky. A magnificent golden eagle was soaring high above the ship. 'Sir,' he exclaimed, 'I hope this is an excellent omen and promises good things to us. The king of birds is come to welcome Your Royal Highness upon your arrival to Scotland.'

Their intention was to land on Barra, near the castle of the MacNeill chief, but they discovered that he was away from home and instead they disembarked on the little island of Eriskay, on a stretch of shore known ever afterwards as 'The Prince's Strand'. In the pouring rain, they stumbled up the beach to stop at the first house they saw. It was a low, stone building, a miserable dwelling by their standards, but with true highland hospitality its owner opened the door and welcomed them in. His name was Angus MacDonald, he said, and several other travellers were already sheltering inside from the storm.

The Prince and his gentlemen were hungry, and so Duncan Cameron, their pilot, roasted some flounders for them over the fire, while Charles sat on a little peat stool, laughing at his attempts at cookery and coughing when the wind blew the smoke back through the hole in the roof. He was forced to get up and go to the door from time to time for a breath of air, and at last Angus gave an exclamation of impatience.

'What a plague is the matter with that fellow that he can neither sit nor stand still, and neither keep within nor without doors?' he demanded. The sudden, horrified silence which greeted his question had him gazing round in bewilderment, but the tall stranger in black merely laughed and the others relaxed again.

When the meal was over, Charles anxiously inspected the few beds which were available. He was worried about Sir Thomas, and he wanted to make sure that the sheets were properly aired. That did not please Angus either, and he hastened to point out that his beds were so good that even a prince would not be ashamed to sleep in them. That appeared to satisfy the visitors, and Sir Thomas duly lay down to rest.

Next morning they were all up early, for there was important business to be done and they had worked out their plan of campaign with care. Scotland was divided into two distinct areas. In the lowlands, people lived much as they did in England. There were great

57. The Prince's Strand, Eriskay, where Charles first set foot in Scotland. (Photograph, National Museums of Scotland)

* Old Style

estates with improving landlords, prosperous towns with merchants, lawyers, doctors and tradesmen. The Scottish language was not so different from English and ever since the countries' parliaments had been united almost forty years before, the English influence had been spreading with increased rapidity.

In the highlands, however, it was a different matter. The mountainous, difficult terrain had always made it hard for crown officials to enforce their authority and even in this, the eighteenth century, the clan chiefs enjoyed an unusual amount of power. Nor were they primitive barbarians. They were cultivated, intelligent men, well-educated and widely travelled, many of them as at home in the drawing-rooms of Edinburgh or Paris as they were in their own formidable castles. To their followers, their word was law and although the clansmen's first loyalty might be to the rightful King, they would do nothing unless their chief commanded them.

Charles therefore intended to begin by contacting the chiefs in the Outer Isles before moving on to the mainland. There he would gather his army, march on Edinburgh, make Scotland his own and then advance into England. He expected to encounter no serious opposition, for he had been told how greatly the British longed for his presence and he was convinced that if any of the soldiers were forced to take the field against him, they would soon lay down their arms when they realised that they were facing their rightful Prince.

The first messenger he sent set off for South Uist to bring back Alexander Macdonald of Boisdale, brother of Clanranald, the Macdonald chief. Eagerly, the Prince and his retinue awaited his arrival, anticipating his delighted excitement when he saw the illustrious visitor. Boisdale arrived, knelt before the Prince and kissed his hand, but his manner was far from triumphant. Instead, he stared grimly at Charles for a long moment and then he said abruptly, 'You must return home'. At these words, everyone was 'struck as if with a thunderbolt'. This was the last reaction they had expected.

'I *am* come home, Sir!' Charles retorted proudly, 'and I will entertain no notion at all of returning to that place from whence I came, for that I am persuaded my faithful Highlanders will stand by me!'

Even that did not shame Boisdale into compliance, and when word was sent to two other leading Jacobites in the locality they too refused to have anything to do with the intended rising.

The Prince was astonished. Summoning a council of war, he discovered to his dismay that, in the face of this unexpected setback, most of his gentlemen were ready to return to France. Only Colonel O'Sullivan and Antoine Walsh were in favour of continuing. Charles debated the matter hotly. He would not hear of an ignominious retreat. They would go on, he insisted, and because he was their Prince they had to agree. Late that same evening they set off to sail the sixty miles to the mainland.

At four o'clock the following afternoon they arrived in Loch nan Uamh, a sea loch just north of Moidart, and Charles and his 'seven men of Moidart' went ashore at Borradale in Arisaig, a wild, bleak

place made even more unwelcoming by the lashing rain. Passing themselves off as smugglers, they sought temporary refuge in a small cottage, sending out messages to the local chiefs, and on 26 July, as the logbook of the *Du Teillay* put it, 'conversations began'. One by one, leading members of the Macdonald family came aboard with their retainers. They were greeted by the Marquis of Tullibardine, who was standing at the entrance to a large tent which had been erected on the deck. Although he had not been in Scotland for thirty years, some of them remembered him and there were emotional reunions. Inside the tent, a table had been set up, with glasses and bottles of brandy. There the clansmen would wait while their leaders saw the Prince in his cabin.

A highlander who was present that day later told how 'There entered the tent a tall youth of a most agreeable aspect, in a plain black coat with a plain shirt, not very clean, and a cambric stock fixed with a plain silver buckle'. On his head was a fair wig, his black hat was attached by a cord to one of his coat buttons and with his black stockings he wore shoes with brass buckles. He was introduced as being an Irish priest and yet there was an indefinable air of authority about him which made them all wonder. It was, of course, the Prince.

For his part, Charles was curious to see at last these highlanders about whom he had heard so much. He gazed in fascination at their strange, unfamiliar apparel: the plaids and the kilts, not made up in the bright garish colours of modern tartan but in soft subdued shades

58. Loch nan Uamh, where the Prince landed on the mainland on 25 July 1745.
(Scottish Tourist Board)

59. *Donald Cameron of Lochiel*, painted some twenty years after his death, by Sir George Chalmers.
(Sir Donald Cameron of Lochiel, KT)

derived from the local dyes and designed to give camouflage against the rough grass and heather. They spoke Gaelic to each other, but the chiefs could converse in English, too, and in spite of their fierce aspect they seemed courteous and deferential. As he would discover, they had their own strict code of honour and an overwhelming pride in their lineage. 'Do you not feel the cold in your highland garb?' Charles asked one man, but he just laughed. He was so used to it, he replied, that anything else would seem strange.

Diverting though these exchanges might be, the conversations in the Prince's cabin were what really mattered and they were not going well. The visitors were extremely polite, even awestruck, when they realised the identity of their host. They knelt before him and kissed his hand, many of them with tears in their eyes, but they all gave him the same advice. He must return to France. He should never have come to Scotland in the first place without an army.

Their dilemma was very real. They felt bound to support him, but they were convinced that the time was not right. They had so much to

lose, not only their possessions but their very lives, yet the Prince was so enthusiastic, so confident and so convincing that in spite of all their reservations they found themselves promising to help.

One of their number was yet to come, however, and he was the most influential of all. Donald Cameron of Lochiel, 'the Gentle Lochiel', might have his financial problems but he was widely respected for his intelligence and his good judgment. He was reluctant to see the Prince at all, but at last he came. There was no witness to what passed between the two men, but John Home, the government historian who lived at the time, went to great trouble to find out the truth of what happened during the campaign, and he is usually a reliable informant. According to him, Lochiel knelt, kissed the Prince's hand and spoke in quiet but resolute tones.

60. *Antoine Walsh leaving for France*, receiving from Charles a letter to James III praising his efforts on behalf of the Prince. Painted by an unknown artist, this picture belonged to Walsh. (Engraving on loan to the Scottish National Portrait Gallery from the National Library of Scotland)

His Highness should not have come. Without an army, the cause was lost before it even began. Charles interrupted, eagerly describing how Louis XV would send assistance as soon as he saw that Scotland was ready to rise. Lochiel remained unimpressed. In the end, reluctant to withhold his co-operation altogether, he suggested that if Charles agreed to stay hidden for some weeks he would sound out his friends about what could be done. The Prince's quick temper flared up at once.

'In a few days', he snapped, 'with the few friends that I have, I will erect the royal standard and proclaim to the people of Britain that Charles Stuart is come over to claim the crown of his ancestors, to win it or perish in the attempt.' He concluded disdainfully, 'Lochiel, who, my father has often told me, was our foremost friend, may stay at home and learn from the newspapers the fate of his Prince!'

That had the desired effect. 'No!' cried Lochiel, 'I will share the fate of my Prince and so shall every man over whom nature or fortune hath given me any power!' The die was cast. Lochiel had given his promise. Now the other chiefs would come in too. The rising could begin.

Charles ordered Walsh to unload his supplies and return to France. He then sent messages to leading Jacobites all over Scotland announcing that he would raise his father's standard at Glenfinnan on 19 August. After that, he composed a letter to Louis XV, telling him that on his arrival he had found 'much good will'. If Louis would send even a modest amount of help, the Prince would soon be in a position not only to take Scotland but to march into England itself.

As he sat writing this letter, far away in Rome his father was receiving news of his expedition. At first he was horrified. This was the very sort of rash behaviour he had dreaded. However, upon reflection, he could not but feel a growing sense of pride.

'If I had been acquainted with it in time I had certainly done my best to prevent it being executed', he told the Earl Marischal, but 'if it was rash, I cannot but say it is a bold undertaking and the courage and sentiments the Prince expresses on this occasion will always do him honour.' Word had not only reached Rome, of course. London too had heard the surprising news and on 1 August the British government placed a price of £30,000 on Charles's head.

For the next fortnight, the Prince remained in the Borradale area, busily planning his campaign: sending out messages, interviewing visitors, supervising the distribution of weapons and food and impressing everyone with his energy and his hard work. His supporters were active too, the chiefs raising their clansmen and a small group of highlanders capturing a government engineer and some soldiers on their way to one of the forts. Finally, all was in readiness and the Prince moved westwards to Glenfinnan, on Loch Shiel.

It was 19 August 1745. Exhilarated though he was, the first sight of that beautiful, isolated loch gave him pause, for its shores seemed utterly deserted. There was no sign of the Macdonalds and the Camerons who had promised to assemble there. Two hours dragged

61. Glenfinnan, at the head of Loch Shiel, where the standard was raised. The monument was erected a hundred years later.
(National Trust for Scotland)

slowly by as Charles eagerly scanned the surrounding hillsides for some sign of life. It was a nerve-racking wait, but at last, in the early afternoon, they spotted a movement high on one of the slopes and, sure enough, two long columns of highlanders began to come slowly down a steep, zigzag path. Lochiel and Macdonald of Keppoch were at their head and between the two lines there walked the disconsolate figures of the captured engineer and redcoats. Estimates of the forces varied, but it seems that Lochiel had about 800 men, Keppoch a further 400 or so.

When they had all assembled at the head of the loch, a solemn ceremony took place. The Marquis of Tullibardine slowly raised the standard of James III and proudly held it aloft, a man standing on either side to support him. Twice the size of any ordinary flag, it was a square of plain white silk, edged with a broad inner border of red and a narrow outer border of blue. While it fluttered proudly in the breeze, James III was proclaimed King and his commission of regency to Charles was read out. After that, the Prince made a moving speech,

praising the loyalty of those present and declaring that it was his duty to procure their welfare just as it was theirs to assert his right. He well knew, he concluded, that they were all ready to join with him in 'so glorious an enterprise'. That evening, they drank his father's health and feasted on meat, cheese and butter.

For the next two days he remained at Loch Shiel. Reports indicated that the Scottish authorities were about to counter his rising and he wanted to know precisely what was intended. George II was on the continent with his army and the administration was in the hands of the principal law officers, led by the able, energetic Lord President of the Court of Session, Duncan Forbes of Culloden. He, it seemed, was determined to crush any insurrection at the very start and he was sending north the small force at his disposal: an army of less than 4000 men, many of them inexperienced and ill-equipped, commanded by Sir John Cope. They were making for Fort Augustus, one of the

63. Caricature believed to
show Sir John Cope, by
George, 1st Marquess of
Townshend. This is the
only known contemporary
picture of him.
(National Portrait Gallery,
London)

government strongholds in the north. In order to get there they would
have to go through the notorious Pass of Corrieyairack, an ideal place
for a Jacobite ambush. Eager to do battle, Charles set off at a rapid
pace, covering as much as twenty miles a day in pouring rain.

Meanwhile, Cope pressed wearily onwards. Lord President Forbes
had assured him that he could easily defeat the Young Pretender and
his handful of supporters, but he was not so sure. Apart from the
unsatisfactory condition of his own men, he was having to carry north
with him 1000 sets of weapons to distribute among those highlanders
who came forward to enlist in his army. The arms were heavy and
cumbersome, his men were tiring rapidly and to make matters worse,
not one volunteer had appeared to join him by the time he reached
Crieff. The countryside ahead was rough and mountainous. It was not
worth trying to take the arms any further and so he sent them back to
Stirling.

From Crieff he travelled to Dalwhinnie and there he found awaiting
him a letter from the Lord President. The next part of the journey
would be the most dangerous, he was warned, for the Pass was not
the only likely source of trouble. The wild, isolated country beyond
was just as perilous and he must be on the lookout all the time for an
enemy trap. As he gazed at his weary, ill-trained troops, Cope's heart
sank. He summoned a council of war and he and his officers reached
an important decision. Instead of climbing up through Corrieyairack
they would turn eastwards and go to the government barracks at
Ruthven. From there, they could move to Inverness.

As a result, when the Prince arrived at Corrieyairack, he found that
the enemy had gone. He and his men were bitterly disappointed, but

64. Loch Eil. Charles
travelled eastwards along
the loch on his way from
Glenfinnan to
Corrieyairack.
(Scottish Tourist Board)

at least the departure of Cope meant that the way to Edinburgh was clear. No army lay between the Jacobites and the capital. For the time being, the inevitable confrontation was postponed and they could concentrate on marching south.

After the 1715 rising, General George Wade had built a network of roads through the highlands so that the government forces would have easy access to those troublesome areas. Now it was a simple matter for the Prince and his men to use them, marching rapidly southwards through Perthshire to Blair Atholl. This was the ancestral territory of the Marquis of Tullibardine. At his approach, his Hanoverian brother the Duke of Atholl departed southwards and the local tenants flocked out to welcome back their long lost landlord. Triumphantly he took possession of Blair Castle, his family home, and there the Prince spent the next few days.

Mrs Robertson of Lude, from a nearby estate, came to act as his hostess and Charles enjoyed a little leisure. He strolled through the garden and said he was intrigued by a large stretch of grass. What was its purpose? It was a bowling green, he was told, whereupon he was even more interested. An English admirer had once sent him a set of bowls, but he had never seen the game played. The following day, he paid a visit to Mrs Robertson's own mansion-house and enjoyed some

lighthearted entertainment. He was even gracious enough to take part in some minuets and a few highland reels.

The music and the dancing, unfamiliar as they were, may have reminded him of the Muti Palace, but his life was now strangely different. To please his followers he had taken to wearing highland dress, not a kilt but tartan trews and a plaid. He also made a point of marching on foot at the head of his little army, instead of riding as a royal general might be expected to do.

In other ways, however, his exalted status was carefully preserved. He had with him his own grooms, his cook and his valet, his silver

65. *Field Marshal George Wade*, probably by Johan van Diest. In the background his men are building the road through the Pass of Corrieyairack. (Scottish National Portrait Gallery)

66. Distant view of Blair
Castle, home of the dukes
of Atholl, visited by
Charles on his way south
and again later.
(Photograph, National
Museums of Scotland)

cups, his elaborate medicine chest and his trunks full of elegant
clothes. Whenever possible, he lodged in large and well-appointed
houses, occupying the best suite of rooms. If no proper accommodation was available, he was perfectly happy to lie down on the
ground with his men, but they saw to it that he had a bed of heather,
as a mark of status as well as for comfort. However willing he was to
identify himself with the clansmen, neither he nor they would have
thought it right if he had lived in the same conditions as themselves.

After the agreeable interlude at Blair, Charles marched on to
Dunkeld and so to Perth, a pleasant town on the banks of the River

67. Late seventeenth-
century engraving of
Perth, on the banks of the
Tay, by John Slezer.
(From *Theatrum Scotiae*:
photograph, Royal
Commission on Ancient
Monuments, Scotland)

Tay. They were leaving the highlands now. The lowlands lay ahead, so he decided to stop for a few days to organise his men. He also took the opportunity of writing to his father to report on his success thus far.

'Sir,' he began, 'Since my landing, everything has succeeded to my wishes. It has pleased God to prosper me hitherto even beyond my expectations. I have got together 1300 men and am promised more brave, determined men who are resolved to die or conquer with me.' It was true that the enemy had eluded them at Corrieyairack, but he was 'not at all sorry for it. I shall have the greater glory in beating them when they are more numerous and supported by their dragoons'.

As for his own little army, discipline, harmony and mutual consideration prevailed to an astonishing degree and every day he had cause to reflect upon his father's parting advice to him. Just as James had said, he found that the exercise of power, 'if tempered with justice' was 'an easy thing to myself and not grievous to those under me'. By keeping to this rule and by 'my conformity to the customs of these people' he could safely say 'I have got their hearts to a degree not to be easily conceived by those who do not see it'.

He was nervous in case his father might contemplate making terms on his behalf with George II and he begged him to put any such thought from his mind. He was determined to continue his campaign. Twice comparing himself to the Black Prince, he begged his father not to be uneasy about him. 'If I die it shall be as I lived, with honour, and

the pleasure I take in thinking I have a brother in all respects more worthy than myself to support your just cause . . . makes life more indifferent to me.' James had always preferred Henry, and Charles knew it. Nor was the apparently fraternal feeling among his men unmarred by jealousy: even his choice of generals caused trouble.

One of those who came to him in Perth was James Drummond, Duke of Perth. Ten years older than Charles, tall, pale and slender, he had been educated on the continent and the Prince took to him right away. His title, his family's devotion to the house of Stuart and his own outstanding courage made him an obvious candidate for

69. *Lord George Murray*, lieutenant-general of the Jacobite army, by an unknown artist.
(The Duke of Atholl at Blair Castle: photograph, *Scotland's Story*)

command. Unfortunately, he was delicate. A childhood accident when he had been crushed by a barrel had left him with breathing problems and digestive troubles. He could only tolerate a milky diet and his friends were worried that his health would never stand up to a campaign. He laughed off their fears, and because he had such a remarkably sweet disposition they did not like to point out that he had little real military experience. As a result, when Charles gave him the position of lieutenant-general they did not protest.

The Prince could not, however, pass over the other principal contender for the position, the Marquis of Tullibardine's brother, Lord

70(*a*) The Prince's seal on the blank commission, showing the Royal Arms as used by the Stuarts, with the Order of the Garter and the Thistle. (National Museums of Scotland)

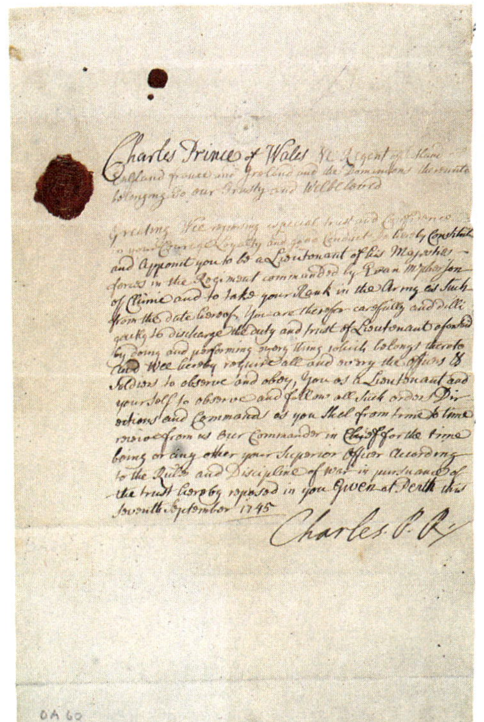

Charles Prince of Wales &c Regent of ye Kingdoms of England France and Ireland and the Dominions thereunto belonging To our Trusty and Wellbeloved

Greeting Wee reposing especial trust and Confidence in your Courage Loyalty and good Conduct Do hereby Constitute and Appoint you to be a Lieutenant of his Majesties forces in the Regiment commanded by Evan McpherJon of Clunie and to take your Rank in the Army as Such from the date hereof You are therefore carefully and diligently to discharge the duty and trust of Lieutenant aforesaid by doing and performing every thing which belongs thereto And Wee hereby require all and every the officers & Soldiers to observe and obey You as ye Lieutenant and yourself to observe and follow all Such orders Directions and Command as you Shel from time to time receive from us Our Commander in Chieff for the time being or any other your Superior officer according to the Rules and Discipline of War in pursuance of the trust hereby reposed in you Given at Perth this Seventh September 1745
Charles P R

70. Blank commission signed by Charles at Perth in September 1745. It was given to MacPherson of Cluny, who was raising forces for the Prince. (National Museums of Scotland)

George Murray. Lord George was a man of a very different nature. Tough, energetic and knowledgeable, he had made the army his career after being exiled for his participation in the '15 and his military prowess was renowned throughout Europe. 'My boys, I don't ask you to advance before me but only to follow me', he would shout as he led his men into battle, and at night he would wrap himself in his plaid and lie down on the ground beside them. 'The true man', they called him in Gaelic.

His arrival in Perth surprised those who had thought that he had developed government sympathies, but the Scottish Jacobites welcomed him warmly for here at last was the professional commander they needed. The Prince and his Irish gentlemen were not so sure. Lord George was polite enough, it was true, but his manner could hardly be called deferential. Even one of his best friends had to admit that he could be 'fierce, haughty and blunt' and another said that he 'desired always to dictate everything by himself and, knowing none his equal, did not wish to receive his advice'. Lord George was impatient when less skilled officers tried to tell him what to do and he could not hide the fact that he thought the Prince young, untried and in no position to plan a campaign.

For his part, Charles found Lord George's censorious air all too reminiscent of his own father. For months now he had been delightfully free from any parental figure telling him what to do. He had no intention of reverting to the position of the meek, obedient son,

71. Advertisement promising £30,000 to anyone 'who secures the son of the Pretender'. Published in Edinburgh in 1745.
(Scottish National Portrait Gallery)

but he could not do without Lord George and so he made him his major-general. That in itself provoked a storm. As soon as Lord George discovered that the Duke of Perth had been accorded a superior rank, he complained bitterly and Charles had to make him a lieutenant-general too. Attempting to avoid future difficulties, he decreed that, in the event of a battle, the Duke and Lord George would have the same number of men each. They would have alternate command of the right and left wings of the army and they would enjoy supreme command day about. That seemed to satisfy them for the time being, but by now the clan chiefs were squabbling over their respective positions and in the end the Prince had to resort to getting them to draw lots.

Despite these quarrels, there was much cause for satisfaction. The Jacobite army was increasing daily and the total had reached over 2000. Moreover, their numbers included various influential figures. Lord Ogilvy had appeared. He had known the Prince in Rome, and there were useful people like Laurence Oliphant of Gask and the Chevalier Johnstone.

A further source of gratification was the arrival of two letters from the continent. One was from Charles's uncle, the Duke of Bouillon, assuring him that Louis XV was preparing to send military assistance.

72. *David, Lord Ogilvy*, by
Allan Ramsay. He was just
twenty when the rising
began.
(In a Scottish private
collection)

The other was from the Spanish ambassador in Flanders giving similar promises of help from his royal master.

News of the Jacobite advance had made an excellent impression in Paris and Madrid. In Edinburgh it caused panic. With only a small garrison in the castle under an aged commander, one regiment of dragoons and a poorly trained local militia to guard them, the prosperous, largely Hanoverian citizens of the capital were realising with a chilling certainty that they had little defence against the inevitable attack. They were sending urgent messages to Cope, begging him to return by sea and protect them, but they feared that he could not come in time. Every five minutes people were looking up at their weathercocks trying to see if the wind was in the right direction.

On 11 September the Prince marched out of Perth. He would go south to the River Forth, cross it near Stirling and then turn east. On his way, his Scottish subjects made sure that he did not miss the famous sites of their country's history. He was taken to Scone, for example, to see where his ancestors had been crowned. As he had anticipated, his advance was largely unopposed. The government soldiers guarding a ford a few miles west of Stirling fled at his approach, and the Jacobites crossed with ease. 'The Young Chevalier', said Scotland's leading newspaper *The Caledonian Mercury*, 'had been the first who put foot in the water and waded through the Forth at the head of his detachment.'

By this time they were relatively near Glasgow, and so the Prince wrote to the provost demanding that the city should contribute £15,000 to his cause as well as handing over all their weapons. They proved unco-operative. Next day, he passed Stirling Castle. As he did so, the government garrison fired their guns at him. Some of the cannonballs fell dangerously near him, but no one was hurt. Stopping at Bannockburn House and Callendar House he reached Linlithgow,

73. Linlithgow Palace, where Charles spent Sunday, 15 September, on his way to Edinburgh. The following year it was severely damaged by fire while occupied by government soldiers.
(In the care of Historic Buildings and Monuments, SDD, and open to the public)

74. The courtyard of Linlithgow Palace with its sixteenth century fountain.
(In the care of Historic Buildings and Monuments, SDD, and open to the public)

75. Edinburgh Castle,
which was held for
George II throughout the
campaign.
(In the care of Historic
Buildings and
Monuments, SDD, and
open to the public)
(Scottish Tourist Board)

with its ancient royal palace. It was six o'clock on a Sunday morning when he took possession of the town and he asked the local ministers to hold their services as they always did while he spent the day quietly in the palace. Edinburgh was now within easy reach. Next day he got as far as Corstorphine, a little village on the edge of the city, and from there he sent a message ordering the provost to open the gates to him.

Cope had not yet arrived back from the north. When they heard that the Jacobites were at hand, distraught citizens ran about the streets while the provost and magistrates desperately debated what should be done. Some were all for defending themselves while others urged immediate surrender. Even as they argued, another letter arrived from the Prince.

'Being now in a condition to make our way into this capital of His Majesty's Ancient Kingdom of Scotland', he wrote, 'we hereby summon you to receive us as you are in duty bound to do.' He had signed himself 'Charles, Prince Regent'. The provost and the magistrates shuddered in dismay when they saw that signature and they decided that they must play for time. The Prince had taken up his lodgings at a miller's house in Slateford and they sent a deputation there, begging to be allowed until two o'clock that morning to consider their reply. Their request was granted, but when two o'clock came they sent their deputation back to ask for an extension. Cope's fleet had been sighted off the east coast. Perhaps they would yet be saved.

The Prince was none too pleased with their second message and, suspecting their motives, he sent the delegation a curt order telling them to 'get them gone'. As they rode off, he put his own plan into effect. While he waited impatiently, Cameron of Lochiel took 800 men and made his way through the darkness to the very edge of the city. Silently, they crept past the castle, so close that they could hear the sentries on guard-duty calling to each other. Undetected, they moved cautiously round the outside of the city wall until they reached one of the main entrances, the Netherbow Gate.

While they remained hidden, one of their number, muffled up like a traveller, advanced and banged loudly on the gate, demanding entrance. The guards would not let him in. Lochiel held a whispered conference with his officers. What was to be done? They were on the point of withdrawing when they heard a sudden clatter and the gate creaked open. The coach which had brought back the provost's deputation was returning to its stables outside the city walls. As it came through, Lochiel and his men rushed in and overpowered the sentries. Within minutes, the capital was theirs and not one drop of blood had been shed.

76. The Netherbow Gate, which stood at the present junction beside the Tron Kirk in Edinburgh. (Royal Commission on Ancient Monuments, Scotland)

5
PRESTONPANS

NEXT MORNING, the Prince dressed with care. He selected a tartan coat with the star of the Order of the Thistle decorating the breast. With this he put on red velvet breeches and long riding boots. His valet buckled his silver-hilted broadsword at his waist and into his belt he tucked a pair of pistols. His own red hair was concealed by a fair wig and on his head he wore a velvet bonnet sewn with gold lace and trimmed with the Jacobite emblem, the white rose. Thus attired, he mounted a magnificent bay horse which the Duke of Perth had given him and rode off for his palace of Holyrood with the Duke at one side, Lord Elcho at the other.

When he entered the palace park a deafening cheer went up and he realised that hundreds of men, women and children had come to see him. The townspeople might have been supporters of George II but curiosity had brought them out to stare at this descendant of their Stuart kings. They pushed and jostled forward, trying to touch his horse's harness, eager to kiss his hand. Even John Home, the historian, who was in the crowd that day as a young government volunteer, had to admit afterwards that 'the figure and presence of Charles Stuart were not ill-suited to his lofty pretensions'.

78. Tartan coat said to have been worn by the Prince. The trews belong to a different outfit. (National Museums of Scotland)

77. The royal park at Holyrood where Charles arrived in triumph on 17 September 1745. (Reproduced by gracious permission of Her Majesty The Queen: photograph National Museums of Scotland)

As the crowd surged forward the Prince was forced to dismount, and he stood for a few moments, gravely acknowledging their cheers. Their enthusiasm was no surprise to him. He had always believed that as soon as they saw their rightful Prince they would return to their proper allegiance. When he eventually arrived at Holyroodhouse, an elderly gentleman stepped forward from the crowd, raised his sword in salute and escorted him ceremoniously into his palace. Preceded by this impromptu escort, Charles climbed the stairs, walked down the Long Gallery and entered the apartments of the hereditary keeper, the Duke of Hamilton. There he would lodge throughout his stay in Edinburgh.

An hour later, trumpets sounded at the Market Cross and the reluctant heralds in their tabards proclaimed James as King of Scots. The committed Hanoverians in the crowd remained grimly silent but the Jacobites cheered wildly and in the tall houses opposite, ladies leaned from the windows to flutter white handkerchiefs.

Throughout the rest of that day, more and more people crowded into the forecourt at Holyrood, hoping for a glimpse of the Prince. He

did appear at a window, but he had a preoccupied air. He was busy meeting a new group of supporters, including Lord Nairne, the Earl of Kellie and William Hamilton of Bangour, the famous poet. Hardly had he spoken with them when word came that Cope had landed at Dunbar. 'Has he, by God!' Charles exclaimed tersely. He knew that he would not have to wait long now for his much desired confrontation with the enemy.

The following morning, Cope set off for Edinburgh. He had only just over 2000 men with him but they made a brave sight as they wound their way through the countryside. First came the cavalry, then the infantry, then the cannon and finally the baggage carts. Their procession was several miles long and the local folk came out to marvel at the unlikely spectacle of an army marching through the fertile fields of East Lothian.

Back in Holyroodhouse, the Prince was holding a council of war, questioning the chiefs anxiously about how their men would behave when they met the redcoats on the field of battle. It was difficult to predict, said Macdonald of Keppoch, for the clansmen had little experience of warfare, but he had no doubt that they would follow their leaders valiantly. When he heard that, Charles was delighted.

'I will lead them myself and charge at their head!' he cried. His horrified companions had great difficulty in convincing him that he must not consider doing that. He was their Prince. His life was precious. If anything happened to him, all would be lost. So determined was he that they had to threaten to resign and go home, before he was finally persuaded not to fight in the front line.

The Jacobite army was drawn up at Duddingston, another village on the edge of Edinburgh, and on 20 September the Prince stood in front of his men, drew his sword and said loudly, 'Gentlemen, I have flung away the scabbard! With God's assistance, I don't doubt of making you a free and happy people. Mr Cope shall not escape us as he did in the Highlands!'

With that, he led them eastwards in a long column, three abreast, the Camerons in front. He was marching at their head once more, no longer in his princely garments but dressed like an ordinary soldier with a coarse plaid over his coat and breeches and a blue bonnet on his head.

They found the enemy drawn up in a large field inland from the villages of Prestonpans and Port Seton. The highlanders would have fallen upon them at once, but the Prince and Lord George wanted to reconnoitre their position first and they soon saw that Cope had the advantage. Behind him, to the north, was the estuary of the River Forth. To the west were high stone park walls. South of him lay a ditch some twelve feet broad and to his east was a wide stretch of marsh. It would be impossible to attack him from any direction without suffering serious casualties.

82. *John, Lord Nairne*, one of those who joined the Prince at Holyrood. (The Duke of Atholl, at Blair Castle)

83. *William Hamilton of Bangour*, the Jacobite poet, by Gavin Hamilton. (Scottish National Portrait Gallery)

It was 20 September and the sun would set at six o'clock. It would be folly to fight in the darkness and so they decided to wait. That night the Prince, Lord George and the Duke of Perth lay down to rest in a field of newly harvested pease. The weather was cold now, with a touch of frost, and as they dozed uneasily, their plaids wrapped tightly round them, a local landowner came up asking to speak to Lord George. He often went shooting on the marsh, he explained, and he knew a safe way across. If they followed him, they could surprise Cope from the east.

Lord George and the Prince were delighted. Having made sure that the man was speaking the truth, they moved out the front line. 1200 men crept stealthily through the night, over the marsh and across the ditch, to take up their position facing the enemy. The Macdonalds were on the right, the Camerons on the left.

When they were all in position, the Prince followed with his second line, consisting of 600 or so soldiers, many of them equipped only with

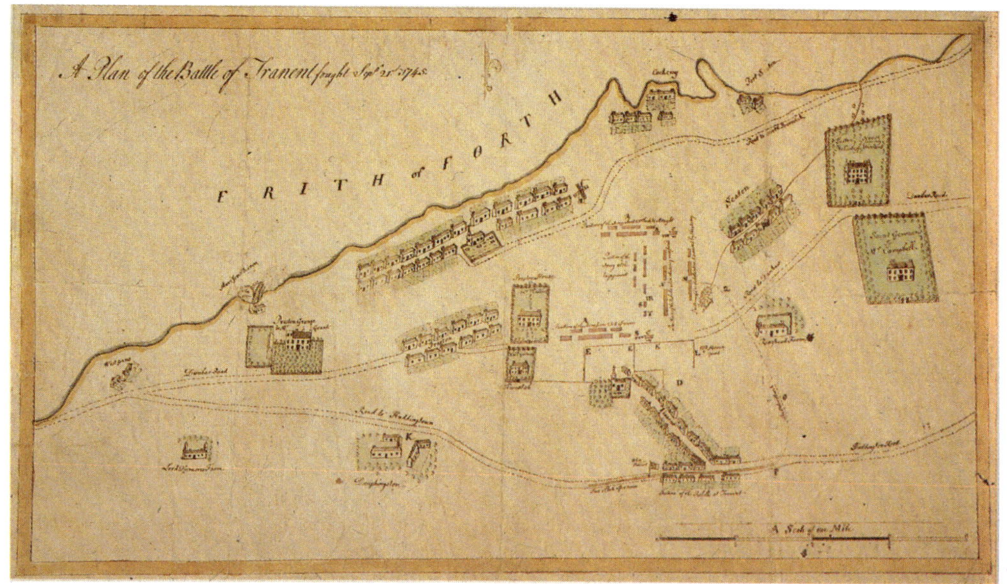

sickles and scythes tied to sticks. Even as they were crossing the marsh, the first line began to advance. A thick mist was swirling round them, hiding them from the enemy. Pulling off their bonnets, the Jacobites said a brief prayer and then, urging each other on and muttering under their breath, they began to run. The newly cut stubble crackled and rustled beneath their feet as they pounded on. Fifty paces behind hurried the second line, trying in vain to catch up. Suddenly, when they were halfway across the field, the sun came out and they could see Cope's forces drawn up before them.

The government soldiers were taken completely by surprise. In fact, when they first saw the Jacobites in the distance, they thought that they were looking at a row of bushes. A moment later, they realised the truth and they fired off their alarm gun. By then it was too late. The Prince's left wing were upon them. When the clansmen sent over a hail of musket-fire, Cope's raw young gunners turned and fled. Their colonel stayed bravely at his post and managed to fire off a salvo himself. For a moment the Jacobite line seemed to shake, but the highlanders kept on going, faster and faster.

A troop of government dragoons came forward to attack, but under the enemy musket-fire they turned and fled. A second troop thundered up, only to reel back in face of their retreating companions. In the ensuing chaos, Cope's infantry panicked. The Jacobites then threw down their muskets and fell upon the enemy, slashing at horses and men alike in a savage attack. As they did so, the final troop of dragoons advanced, wavered and fled. Within seven or eight minutes it was all over. The Prince had routed his enemies at the battle of Prestonpans.

Mounting his horse, Charles stopped the slaughter at once, shouting 'Make prisoners! Spare them! Spare them! They are my

84. Plan of the battle of Prestonpans, here called the Battle of Tranent. (National Library of Scotland)

father's subjects!' Even so, the bodies of the dead were piled seven and eight deep beside the park walls, and Charles was horrified to see that no one was caring for casualties. When his friends urged him to leave the scene he said at once, 'No, I can't rest until I see my own poor men taken care of, and the other wounded too, for they are the King's subjects as well as we and it is none of their fault if they are led on blindly'.

He instructed the Duke of Perth to see that the wounded were taken to the infirmary in Edinburgh and insisted on supervising personally the arrangements for burying the dead. Not until the morning was well advanced did he pause for any refreshment, taking a little meat and some wine from a small table set up beside the captured enemy cannon. He finally left the battlefield at noon.

Optimistic as Charles had been about the outcome, even he was astonished by the speed and the completeness of his success. It was, he wrote to his father, 'one of the most surprising actions that ever was. We gained a complete victory over General Cope, who commanded three thousand foot and two regiments of the best

dragoons in the island, he being advantageously posted, with also batteries of cannon and mortars, we having neither horse nor artillery with us . . . Only our first line had occasion to engage, for actually in five minutes the field was cleared of the enemy, all the foot killed, wounded or taken prisoner and of the horse only two hundred escaped like rabbits, one by one. On our side we only lost a hundred men between killed and wounded, and the army afterwards had a fine plunder'.

While Charles spent the rest of that day resting at Pinkie House nearby, Cope was riding frantically for the border. He did not stop until he reached Berwick, where Lord Mark Kerr congratulated him sardonically on being the first general in history to bring news of his own defeat. About 400 of his dragoons had escaped with him while another 100 fled in the opposite direction to find refuge in Edinburgh Castle. Over 300 of his men were dead. Almost all the rest, including four or five hundred wounded, had been taken prisoner. The Prince had lost fewer than forty men, with eighty or so injured.

Charles would dearly have liked to pursue Cope south, but his army had scattered with their booty and so instead he returned to Edinburgh to scenes of great rejoicing. He himself was strangely sombre. The enemy army had consisted of English and Scots and he was, he explained, 'far from rejoicing at the death of any of his father's subjects'. The men he had defeated were not really his adversaries. He 'pitied their unhappy way of thinking, which had drawn so many misfortunes upon the country and ended in their own fall', but he would think it 'unnatural in his followers to make public rejoicings upon the deaths of their own countrymen'.

86. Satirical engraving showing Cope fleeing to Berwick.
(National Library of Scotland, on loan to the Scottish National Portrait Gallery)

EVERSO MISSUS
SUCCURRERE SECLO

Charles had learned well the lessons of his youth. Humanity, moderation and mercy were the qualities he must cultivate, James had told him time and again, and apart from that he was conscious that once he was Regent of Britain there would be a need for reconciliation.

His officers were taken aback, and they soon discovered that there was another, much more serious difference in outlook between themselves and the Prince. Not only did Charles continue to press for the pursuit of Cope: he made it plain that London, not Edinburgh, was his true objective, a possibility which most of the clan chiefs had never seriously considered. They had left their lands in the belief that they were restoring the Stuarts to the throne of Scotland. When that was done they would return home, and Charles would rule the country as the independent nation it had once been.

Apart from anything else, the highlanders had no desire to fight on unfamiliar territory. They liked to stay within easy reach of their own homes and they had no knowledge of the techniques of lowland warfare. They might have won at Prestonpans, but the chiefs knew that facing a properly trained army in the English countryside would be a very different matter.

Even those who agreed with Charles were forced to point out that, incomplete as their army now was, they could not possibly set out yet. Too many of the clansmen had gone home with their booty. They would return, but not for some weeks. The Prince could not but agree and so it was decided that they should remain in Edinburgh for the time being. Charles could at least console himself with the thought that far more people would flock to him now that his victory was common knowledge, and Louis XV would surely need no more convincing that this was the time to strike.

Resigning himself to the delay, the Prince established a new routine at Holyroodhouse. He was always up before dawn himself, and at nine o'clock the official business of the day began with a meeting of his council in his drawing-room. The council consisted of Perth and Lord George, noblemen like Lord Elcho and Lord Nairne, the various clan chiefs and the Prince's Irish advisers, Sheridan and O'Sullivan. John Murray of Broughton acted as his secretary.

These morning meetings were scarcely peaceful affairs. Lord George and the Duke of Perth treated each other with chilly civility. The Macdonalds and the Camerons were still vying with each other and the Scots were united in their hatred of the Irish. For their part, Colonel O'Sullivan and Sir Thomas Sheridan had no liking for the Scots. The Colonel was constantly telling the Prince that Lord George was not to be trusted, that he was a Hanoverian spy and that he would change sides as soon as the opportunity arose. There was no truth in these accusations, but Charles became increasingly suspicious.

The combination of such conflicting personalities was bound to give trouble, nor did the Prince's own attitude help. At the beginning of each meeting he stated his own point of view and then invited the others to speak, but it was clear to them that he had no intention of taking their advice and indeed he resented any contradiction.

87. *Charles* during his stay at Holyrood, engraved by Sir Robert Strange. This is the only authentic portrait of the Prince dating from his time in Scotland. (Scottish National Portrait Gallery)

*The following ORDER is published by Autho-
rity.*

WHereas it is necessary, for preserving the Regularity of our Army, that all Volunteers that have or may offer their Service to us, join themselves to some Regiment of Foot or Horse, or Train of Artillery, so that they may be mustered, paid, and do Duty alongst with them; We therefore hereby order all the said Volunteers already in our Service, to join as aforesaid, within forty eight Hours after the Publication hereof, and such as shall hereafter offer their Service to us, are to join as aforesaid within forty eight Hours after their Arrival at our Army. And we hereby prohibite and discharge, under our highest Displeasure, any Person or Persons to wear Cockades, unless they be joined as said is, or belong to the Conductors of our Baggage, Forage, Provisions, Houshold, or other Branch of our Service. Given at our Palace of *Holy-rood-house*, the twenty second Day of *October* 1745.

88. Printed order by the Prince while at Holyrood, giving instructions to volunteers joining his army.
(Abercairny Papers, Scottish Record Office. Reproduced by kind permission of W. G. Drummond Moray Esq)

According to Lord Elcho, he 'could not bear to hear anybody differ in sentiment from him and took a dislike to everybody that did, for he had a notion of commanding this army as any general does a body of mercenaries and so let them know only what he pleased'. Part of the trouble was that Charles was anxious to assert his authority over these older, more experienced men and so he tended to brush aside some of the very useful information they gave him.

Determined to rule as he ought, he persevered with his daily councils even though they all too often degenerated into unseemly wrangling. He was uneasily aware that his army had shrunk to half its previous size and he was determined to conceal this situation from enemy spies. He therefore made sure that the remaining troops were scattered through the town. He moved them constantly from one place to the next and in that way he prevented his opponents from counting his total force.

Each afternoon he rode out to the military camp at Duddingston, and his inspections there became a regular social event. Jacobite or Hanoverian, the ladies of Edinburgh thronged to the camp, partly to admire the soldiers but mostly to see the Prince. 'He was sitting in his

tent when I first came to the field', one young Hanoverian girl wrote to tell a friend. 'The ladies made a circle round the tent and after we had gazed our fill at him he came out of the tent with a grace and majesty that is inexpressible. He saluted all the circle with an air of grandeur and affability capable of charming the most obstinate Whig and, mounting his horse, which was in the middle of the circle, he rode off to view the men . . . I never saw so noble nor so graceful an appearance as His Highness made . . . he seems to be cut out for enchanting his beholders and carrying people to consent to their own slavery in spite of themselves.'

Soon all the young women were wearing white cockades, whatever their political persuasion, and they ordered tartan dresses, embroidered Jacobite mottoes on pincushions and garters and sent the Prince presents of plate, linen and other furnishings.

In the evening, they all went down to Holyrood to watch him take supper. Just as he and his parents had dined in public at the Muti Palace, so did he eat before an admiring crowd in his Scottish dining-room. He always dressed elegantly and his manner could not have been more gracious. Hanging on his every word, the ladies did not seem to notice that he had no real interest in any of them. The reaction of the Jacobite Miss Threipland of Fingask was typical of the feelings he evoked. After seeing him at Holyrood one evening she told a friend, 'Oh, had you beheld my beloved Hero, you must confess he is a Gift from Heaven, but then, besides his outward appearance, which is absolutely *the best figure* I ever saw, such Vivacity, such piercing Wit, woven with a clear Judgment and an active Genius and allowed by all to have a Capacity apt to receive such impressions as are not usually stamped on every brain: in short, Madam, he is *the Top of Perfection* and *Heaven's Darling*'.

89. Satirical engraving showing the Scottish ladies flocking round the Prince at Holyrood. Published in January 1746. (The Trustees of the British Museum)

90. The Jacobite symbol, the white rose, was worn by the Prince's followers in the form of a white cockade. This white rose was made by Isabella Lumisden for her future husband, Sir Robert Strange, to wear on the day Charles entered Edinburgh.
(National Museums of Scotland)

91. Fan decorated with a painting of the Prince.
(National Museums of Scotland)

In fact, Charles followed the dictates of court etiquette because he had always done so, but his thoughts were on more important matters. With his singleminded devotion to his own ambitions, he had no time for idle dalliance. He would far rather have snatched a quick bite to eat and gone back to the camp to plan for the days ahead.

He was working so hard that his gentlemen began to feel that a little recreation would not go amiss and they decided to gratify all the ladies who were begging them to hold a ball. They kept it a secret from him, hoping to give him a pleasant surprise. A time was fixed, the ladies and gentlemen of the town came down to the palace in their very best clothes and after they had watched the Prince eat supper in the usual way they waited in pleasurable anticipation. His gentlemen then told him that a special entertainment was about to take place in his honour, and they begged him to attend.

To their dismay, Charles betrayed neither pleasure nor surprise. He merely nodded and said with his usual courtesy that he would go and watch for a little. Excitedly the ladies stepped out on to the dance floor, wondering which of them he would choose as his partner. All their hopes were doomed to disappointment, however. The evening had scarcely begun when he rose, excused himself and strode off to his own apartments.

Some of his gentlemen ran after him, explaining eagerly that the ball had been arranged specially to amuse him. They knew, they said, how fond he had been of dancing in Rome. Surely he would come back and join in, at least for a little while.

'It is very true I like dancing', the Prince replied, 'and am very glad to see the ladies and you divert yourselves, but I have now another air to dance and until that be finished I'll dance no other.'

Nothing they could say would make him change his mind. O'Sullivan and the rest could only shake their heads and marvel that a young prince of his age, who really enjoyed dancing and sport, 'never thought of any pleasures and was as retired as a man of sixty'.

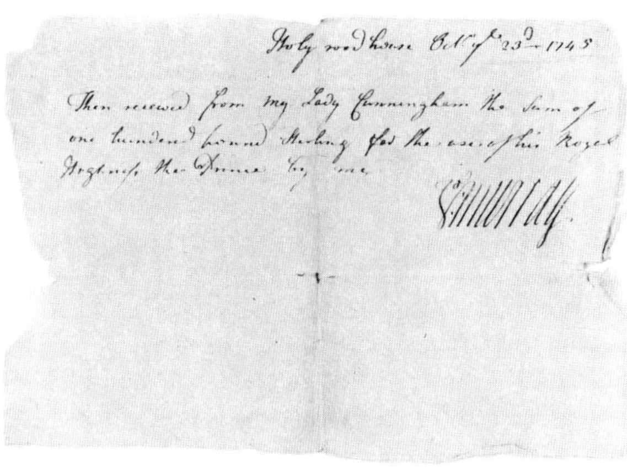

Meanwhile, Charles followed his usual practice and went down to Duddingston to sleep in his tent.

There were so many new developments now, it was hardly surprising that he was preoccupied. News of his victory at Prestonpans was having exactly the effect he had expected. Almost every day new and influential supporters were arriving. At the beginning of October, Lord Pitsligo appeared, bringing with him 132 horse and 248 foot soldiers. A thin, small, fairhaired man more at home in his study than on the battlefield, he was so highly respected by his contemporaries that when he declared himself, many more followed suit.

Lord Lewis Gordon came in and then the master of Strathallan. Cluny MacPherson arrived with the promise of more soldiers and the Earl of Kenmure rode up with his sizeable contingent. The Marquis of Tullibardine had stayed behind in Perthshire to raise his men and Lord George was plying him with a series of impatient letters, telling him to hurry up. Most satisfactory of all, perhaps, was the initiative of the dashing Lord Elcho. He had set about assembling four squadrons of 'gentlemen of character'. Smartly kitted out in blue and red uniforms with lace-bedecked waistcoats, they would serve as Horse Lifeguards, a personal bodyguard for the Prince.

There was also a brief spell of military action in the city itself. Charles, hearing rumours that the government garrison was short of supplies, decided to blockade the castle. This was exactly what the commander wanted. He was determined to prevent the Jacobites from marching south by keeping them occupied where they were. When the blockade began, he retaliated by firing on the Camerons who were stationed at the castle gates, but after several innocent bystanders had been killed, the Prince called off the entire operation.

That brief attempt to starve out the enemy had been a failure, but there was very encouraging news from further north. Help from France had begun to arrive at last. Four French ships carrying men, arms and ammunition had arrived in the ports of Montrose and

92. *David, Lord Elcho,* commander of the Prince's lifeguards, probably by D. Dupra.
(In a Scottish private collection)

93. Receipt for £100 lent to Charles at Holyrood by Lady Cunningham of Caprington. It is signed by his secretary, John Murray of Broughton.
(Dick Cunyngham of Prestonfield Papers, Scottish Record Office)

Stonehaven on the east coast. Aboard the first vessel was a special envoy from Louis XV. Boyer, Marquis d'Eguilles was an able, energetic lawyer and he was full of enthusiasm for his mission. So eager was he, indeed, that when his ship arrived he helped to unload its cargo of weapons, wading ashore with armfuls of guns, oblivious of both comfort and personal dignity. He then rode quickly to Edinburgh to hand the Prince a letter from Louis XV. It was couched in friendly but vague terms. Much more important were the Marquis's personal assurances that Louis was going to act.

What had happened was that, until the end of July, the French ministers had denied all knowledge of the Prince's expedition, but at the end of August Antoine Walsh had arrived back in the *Du Teillay*, with glowing descriptions of the warm welcome which had awaited Charles. When this was swiftly followed by the news that he had entered Edinburgh, the French were suddenly all enthusiasm. Naval and army commanders were ordered to collect both men and arms for service in Scotland and early in October Louis XV ordered the Duke of Perth's brother, Lord John Drummond, to take his French regiment of Royal Scots to help the Jacobite cause.

The very next day, Louis learned of the victory at Prestonpans. The time had come for a full-scale invasion of Britain. Just ten days after the Marquis d'Eguilles was presented to Charles, a secret treaty was signed at Fontainebleau between the Prince's emissary and the representatives of Louis XV. By its terms, the French gave definite undertakings that they would send assistance. The plan was to assemble the sort of invasion force Charles himself had been longing to lead in 1743. Now his brother would take command. No fewer than 12,000 men would sail for England, led by the Duke of Richelieu.

Knowing this, Charles was growing more and more impatient to launch his own invasion of England; all the more so because he had heard that the government were busy with their preparations. Lord President Forbes had been hard at work in the north of Scotland, putting together a small government army to be commanded by Lord Loudon. More ominously, the British army had been recalled from Flanders and each week transport vessels filled with soldiers were sailing into the Thames. On 1 October, George II ordered Field Marshal Wade to march north towards Scotland with a strong body of both cavalry and infantry. Wade was in his seventies now, 'infirm in mind and body, forgetful, irresolute, perplexed, snappish', said one of his own officers. He knew that he was too old for the job and the thought of leading a winter campaign filled him with dismay. However, because of his experience in building the roads and bridges after the 1715 rising, he had an unparalleled knowledge of the Scottish countryside and from that point of view he seemed to be the obvious choice. Reluctantly he set off. By 19 October he was in Doncaster and on the 29th he reached Newcastle. Details of his position came to the Prince the following day, and he summoned a council of war.

As was his custom, he spoke first. The moment of crisis had come, he said. They must march south at once to confront the enemy. The government army might be far larger and far better trained than their own force, but that did not matter. The highlanders had shown at Prestonpans that they were equal to anyone and they had the advantage of being in the peak of condition after their enforced rest in Edinburgh. Wade's men, on the other hand, would obviously be exhausted after their continental campaign, the sea voyage back and the long march from London. No time was to be lost. They should set out at once.

Having said his piece, the Prince sat back and waited for the others to agree with him. Looking at each other uneasily, first one and then another clan chief spoke. As far as they were concerned, they said, they had done what they had intended to do. Scotland was theirs. Apart from driving out a few government garrisons, their mission was accomplished.

The Prince listened to them with growing chagrin. 'I find, Gentlemen, you are for staying in Scotland and defending your country', he said at last. 'I am resolved to go to England.'

Nothing would make him alter his intentions. He 'had his mind only occupied by England', said the Chevalier Johnstone. They seemed to have reached a deadlock and it fell to Lord George Murray to try to find a compromise. Instead of marching to Newcastle to confront the alarmingly large government army, he proposed that they should go to Carlisle. That would give the English Jacobites time to join them and then, thus augmented, they could turn east to meet Wade.

As usual, the clan chiefs were ready to rely on Lord George's judgment. They were distinctly uneasy at the prospect of quitting their native land but if Lord George said it was practicable, they were willing to go along with it. The Prince was not. If they went to Carlisle, he said, it would look as if they were running away; the French would think it not worthwhile helping and would abandon the notion of an invasion. The chiefs did not care about that, and the heated discussion which ensued lasted far into the evening. Finally, the meeting adjourned without any decision having been taken.

The Prince retired to his quarters and there he pondered the problem. Normally, nothing would have persuaded him to change his mind, but he could see that it would be impossible to lead the clansmen south if they were determined not to go. Perhaps Lord George's compromise was the only way he could put his plans into effect. The following morning when his council resumed its meeting he surprised them all by announcing that he was prepared to implement Lord George's proposal. He did not agree with it personally of course, he said, but he would abide by the majority decision. He even had a helpful suggestion of his own to make. In order to confuse the enemy, they should divide their army into two columns. He and Lord George would set off for Carlisle. The Duke of Perth would make a feint towards the east, giving the impression that Newcastle was their true objective. Once over the border, the Duke would march his men west to join the main force at Carlisle. Thus was it agreed. The Jacobites would enter England.

6

ENGLAND

THAT EVENING the Prince left Edinburgh. Halting at Pinkie, Dalkeith and Thirlestane, he reached the River Esk and prepared to cross. With every mile south, the highlanders had become more and more nervous about leaving their native land and 500 of them had deserted before they arrived at the border. When one of the big cannon toppled into the river and a gunner broke a leg trying to retrieve it, their mood grew blacker still. The Esk was not wide and they were soon over it. Reaching the other side, they wheeled round to face their homeland, drew their swords and raised them in salute. As Lochiel unsheathed his, he cut his hand and all who saw felt a thrill of superstitious dread. No good would come of this excursion into foreign territory.

The Prince himself was in high spirits, delighted to be on the move, and the following day the Duke of Perth and his column caught up with them. Their army back at full strength, they marched boldly for Carlisle, their arrival striking terror into the hearts of the English.

As usual, Charles marched at their head, wearing highland dress. Trying to prevent any more bickering, he led a different regiment each day. Elcho's Lifeguards in their colourful uniforms made an impressive sight and there were several other troops of horse as well. Far outnumbering them, however, were the thirteen regiments of infantry. All wore highland dress, although a number of the soldiers were in fact lowlanders, and the local people stared aghast at these alien beings in their kilts and plaids.

The main body of the army took three or four hours to pass and even then the spectacle was not over. There was a long line of more than sixty baggage carts, followed by the twelve surviving cannon, some captured at Prestonpans, the rest brought over from France. Beside them came large herds of black cattle. The Prince and his commanders were determined that there should be no pillaging and looting, and so they had brought along their own food supply. The cattle would be slaughtered when needed. The lengthy cavalcade was completed by several coaches carrying 'the Highland Ladies', Lady Ogilvy, Mrs Murray of Broughton and several other wives who were determined not to miss any of the excitement. There were also the usual camp-followers, straggling along on foot.

The discipline of this apparently barbaric force was excellent. There was indeed no looting, no harrying of the local people and no assaults. Even so, rumours of their savagery spread like wildfire. They were murdering and raping wherever they went, it was said, and, most horrible of all, the clansmen ate children. Those who were forced to encounter the Jacobites at close quarters were astonished to discover that they were human after all.

94. The Bear Gates at Traquair House which, according to tradition, were closed in 1745 after a visit from the Prince, never to be reopened until the Stuarts are restored. (By kind permission of Peter Maxwell Stuart of Traquair House, Innerleithen, Peeblesshire: photograph, Jarrold Colour Publications)

95. Late seventeenth-century engraving of Thirlestane Castle, where Charles spent the night of 3 November 1745 on the way to England, by John Slezer.
(From *Theatrum Scotiae*: photograph, Royal Commission on Ancient Monuments, Scotland)

'Gentlemen', said one old woman ironically to the officers quartered in her house, 'I suppose you have done with your murdering today? I should be glad to know when the ravishing begins!'

Even the Prince had firsthand experience of the general panic when he discovered a little girl hidden below the bed in his lodgings near Carlisle, and her mother begged him hysterically not to kill her. Charles was appalled, and his kindness to the poor woman won him the gratitude of the entire community.

That same day, his advance guard reached a hill opposite Carlisle. The governor of the castle had climbed the cathedral tower to scan the surrounding countryside and he sighted them with a feeling of despair. He could not possibly order his guns to fire on them, for the Martinmas market had been held that day and the lanes were full of country people going home. He dared not risk heavy civilian casualties and in any event he knew that what he saw was a mere fraction of the total enemy army. His plight was desperate. The town walls were in a poor state of repair, his garrison consisted of elderly soldiers and invalids and the local militia had no experience of warfare. He sent a desperate message to Marshal Wade, begging him to come to the rescue.

Next morning, the Prince sent a letter ordering Carlisle to surrender. He fully expected the authorities to open their gates to him, for he remained convinced that the English would never take the field against their rightful Prince. To his indignation, the town officials refused. At that point a fog came down, so thick, said O'Sullivan, that 'a man could hardly see his horse's ears'. It was not possible to start preparing to besiege the city but in the evening the Duke of Perth began to direct the digging of trenches outside the walls. At the same

96. *Margaret, Lady Ogilvy*, painted by Allan Ramsay in Edinburgh in 1745. (In a Scottish private collection)

time, the Prince received the welcome news that Field Marshal Wade intended to come to the relief of Carlisle. Here at last was the opportunity for real action. They should abandon the siege, he told his council, and march to meet the enemy. Wade's men would be wearier than ever, and they would be caught in hilly country ideally suited to the clansmen's mode of attack.

For once, they were all in agreement and the Jacobites moved east to halt at Brompton. Full of enthusiasm, the Prince prepared to do battle. 'After that', he wrote to tell an English supporter, 'we intend to take our route straight for London and if things answer our expectations we design to be in Lancashire before the 24th inst. Then I hope you and all my friends in that country will be ready to join us.' Echoing his father's words on a previous occasion, he concluded, 'For now is the time or never'.

He was up long before dawn the next day and after breakfasting on duck and hot mutton he rode out to select the battlefield. Even as he did so, the weather was ruining all his plans. Snow was falling so heavily in the east that it was lying seven or eight inches deep. Wade

97. Eighteenth-century
engraving of the south-
west prospect of the city of
Carlisle, with the castle on
the left.
(Royal Commission on the
Historical Monuments of
England)

98. Carlisle Market Cross,
where James III was
proclaimed king when the
Jacobite army arrived in
1745.
(Royal Commission on the
Historical Monuments of
England)

could not possibly set out. He was still in Newcastle. There would be no battle in the immediate future.

Determined not to be balked of his military triumph, Charles announced that they should remain in Brompton until Wade arrived. The others were not so sure. They reminded each other gloomily that as yet no English Jacobites had come to join them, and where was the much vaunted French army? Without support from these sources, the enterprise was far too dangerous. Perhaps they should return to Scotland.

In the debate that followed it fell once more to Lord George Murray to devise a practical compromise. The Prince could stay at Brompton with part of the army, he suggested, while he and the others went back and captured Carlisle. Charles agreed. He created a great deal of trouble for himself, however, by telling Lord George that the Duke of Perth would have joint command of the siege. Lord George, that internationally renowned expert in strategy, was furious, and he retorted brusquely that of course he himself knew nothing of such work, infuriating Charles. They parted on the worst of terms.

Seething with resentment, Lord George set about planning operations with his usual skill while the Duke of Perth saw to the digging of the trenches. This was no easy task, for the highlanders regarded manual labour of this kind as being beneath their dignity; nor was the situation improved by the fact that snow was now falling and the temperature was very low. The Duke gallantly decided to set an example, stripped off his coat and seized a spade. The clansmen were immediately shamed into joining him.

Next day, when the people of Carlisle looked out and saw the highlanders digging industriously and cutting down trees for scaling ladders, their hearts failed them. They hung out a white flag and the Duke of Perth went to discuss terms for their surrender. At this, Lord George flew into a fury. It was he who should be receiving the surrender of the enemy, he stormed. Perth was a Catholic. The English would draw the worst possible conclusion from his participation. They would believe that all their fears about the Stuarts were justified. They would think that Charles had come to impose his own religion upon them. Worst of all, his own pride was hurt. Picking up a pen, he dashed off a furious letter to the Prince.

'Sir,' he wrote, 'I cannot but observe how little my advice as a general officer has any weight with Your Royal Highness ever since I had the honour of a commission from your hands. I therefore take leave to give up my commission. But as I ever had a firm attachment to the Royal Family and in particular to the King my Master, I shall go on as a volunteer and design to be this night in the trenches as such.'

He did not think for one moment that Charles would accept his resignation but he had reckoned without the Prince's own fiery temper. Not only did Charles take exception to the disrespectful tone of the letter; what really annoyed him was the reference to Lord George's loyalty to James III, with no mention of Charles himself. It was a studied insult, he believed, and he replied accordingly. He was, he said, 'extremely surprised you should throw up your commission for a reason which I believe was never heard of before. I am glad of your particular attachment to the King', he added sarcastically, 'but I am very sure he will never take anything as proof of it but your deference to me. I accept of your demission as Lieutenant-General and your future services as a volunteer.'

That was a bombshell indeed, and not only to Lord George. As word spread throughout the Jacobite camp, the clan chiefs and their followers were horrified. They declared openly that they would not go on with any other commander. Lord George must be reinstated or they would go home. The Duke of Perth was busy receiving the surrender of Carlisle but as soon as he heard what had happened he realised that there was only one way out of the dilemma. He went to the Prince and said that he would resign instead. Moreover, having heard that Lord Elcho was also on the point of quitting because he was heartily sick of his responsibility for the baggage train, he offered to take over that particularly trying duty. The Prince agreed unwillingly, Lord George stiffly consented to resume his post and peace was restored for the time being. On 18 November 1745 the Prince rode into Carlisle on a white horse, his pipers playing, his army marching behind him. He lodged in the house of Mr Higham, an attorney, in English Street and almost at once he called a council of war. There was still no sign of Wade, so he declared that they should set off for London without delay.

99. The Prince's targe or shield, with elaborate silver decoration, probably presented to him by the Duke of Perth. (National Museums of Scotland)

This produced an immediate outcry. Lord George hastened to point out that the government had not just one army now but three. Marshal Wade was believed to be at Hexham. A second army was moving north towards Coventry and a third force was being assembled to defend London itself. If they marched south, Lord George said, the Jacobites could be trapped between Wade and the second force. With fewer than 4500 soldiers, there was no possibility that the Prince could survive that. Reinforcements were desperately needed and until they came it was only sensible to wait at Carlisle. Once the English Jacobites and the French had come, they could think of making a move.

The Prince's reaction was that they would appear timid, not to say cowardly, if they stayed where they were. As soon as they set out, he declared confidently, the English would join them. So enthusiastic did he seem and so sure of success that once more his council members found themselves convinced against their will. When Charles said that he had letters from the English Jacobites promising to rise and join him

100. The Prince's sword,
with silver basket hilt.
Made in London in 1740–1,
it was sent to him as a gift
and, according to
tradition, fell into
Cumberland's hands after
Culloden.
(National Museums of
Scotland)

at Preston, they argued no further. Dividing into two columns, one led by the Prince, the other by Lord George, they left Carlisle.

Straining every nerve to reach the capital, Charles set himself a punishing schedule. Lord Elcho described afterwards how 'he never dined nor threw off his clothes at night, nor ate much supper: used to throw himself upon a bed at eleven o'clock and was up by four in the morning. As he had a prodigious strong constitution he bore fatigue surprisingly well'. Like his mother, he was indifferent to personal comfort when in pursuit of an ideal, and on a lonely stretch of road between Penrith and Shap he nearly fainted with exhaustion. His driving ambition kept him going even in the most demanding circumstances and he was cheered on by his impression of enthusiasm among the local people.

Whenever his army entered a town his officers rode ahead to arrange a welcome. The inhabitants were compelled to ring bells, light bonfires and put candles in their windows. By the time the Prince arrived, his father's proclamation would have been read out and if the crowds on the streets seemed surly and unresponsive, Charles put this down to the years of oppression they had suffered under the Hanoverians. In their moment of liberation, he thought, they were too surprised and relieved to be able to rejoice openly. That would come later.

Thus deceived, he made his way to Penrith and so to Lancaster. An English spy saw him there, pacing about the gardens of his Church Street lodgings, as usual unable to relax. The man sent a description of

101. The George Hotel, Penrith, where Charles halted from 21–23 November 1745 and again during his retreat. (Royal Commission on the Historical Monuments of England)

102. Flag of the Stewarts of Appin, which was later carried at Culloden. (On loan to the Scottish United Services Museum from The Stewart Society)

him to London. The Pretender's son was 'about five feet eleven inches high, pretty strong and well-built, has a brown complexion, full cheeks and thickish lips that stand out a little. He looks more of the Polish than the Scottish breed. . . .'

Charles was feeling particularly pleased that evening because he had just heard that Lord John Drummond had arrived at Montrose, bringing with him not only his own regiment of Royal Scots but the six detachments of Irish regiments who served in the French army, Fitzjames's Regiment of Horse and several large guns. Lord John had no intention of marching south just yet. He would wait and see how the Prince's English campaign went before he set off to join him. Charles did not know that, of course, and he imagined that the reinforcements would obey his order to come to him immediately.

Full of optimism, he set off for Preston, a significant place in Scotland's history. Twice in the past century her army had been defeated there by the English and the highlanders were apprehensive lest this should be the scene of a third disaster. To show them that the town did not present some intangible barrier, Lord George marched them straight through and out at the other side. They all heaved a sigh of relief and their spirits rose still further as they noticed that people in the area seemed almost friendly. There were even one or two spontaneous cheers at their approach.

Wigan was the next stopping-place and then it was on to Manchester. The people of Manchester had rejoiced openly when they heard about Prestonpans and now they gave the Jacobites a fairly cheerful reception. The army began to enter the town at about eleven o'clock on the morning of 29 November and by the time the Prince appeared at three the bells were ringing, people were cheering and several local notabilities came forward of their own accord to kiss his hand. That night over supper in his lodgings in Market Street Lane, Charles spoke eagerly of his entry into London. How should he arrive,

he asked his companions. Should he ride or walk? Should he wear highland dress or his own court clothes?

The topic was an absorbing one, but even as he sat chatting happily to Sheridan and O'Sullivan, there was grumbling and discontent among the clan chiefs. It was all very well to speak of taking London, but the British were not going to sit back and allow that to happen. George II had appointed his favourite son, the Duke of Cumberland, to take over the second government army and he posed a much more dangerous threat than the aged Field Marshal Wade. He was young, almost the same age as the Prince, and he had real military experience: he had been in Flanders with his father's army. Already he had

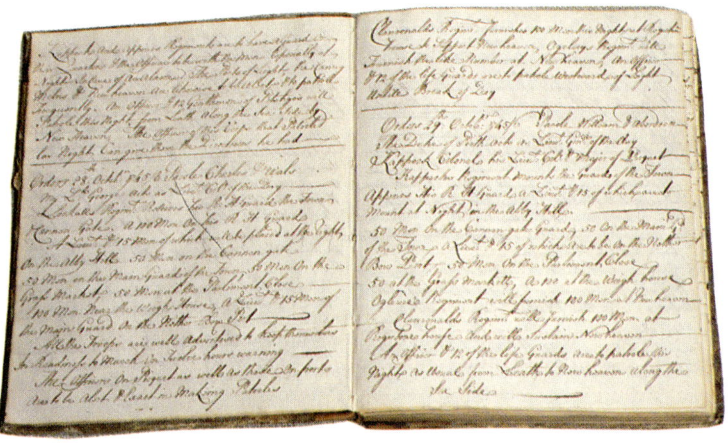

104. Book of orders issued to the Appin Regiment, which formed part of the Jacobite army. The book was compiled soon after the campaign ended. (National Museums of Scotland)

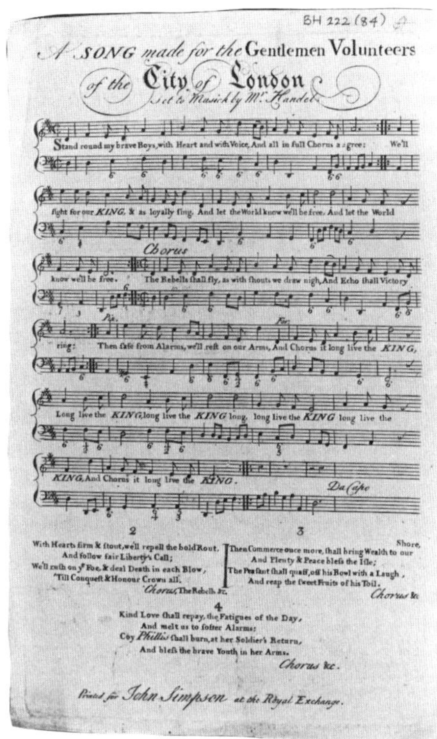

105. 'Stand round, my brave boys', a song composed for the Gentlemen Volunteers who were preparing to defend London against the Jacobites: with music by Handel.
(National Library of Scotland)

something of a reputation for being active, bold and harsh. He would never let the Jacobites overrun the country if he could prevent it.

Most worrying of all was the inertia of the English. It was beginning to look as if they were perfectly happy with Hanoverian rule. That being so, there was no place for a Scottish army in England. The chiefs began to feel that they should never have come south at all. Their help was not desired.

Untroubled by any such misgivings, the Prince rode happily round Manchester the next day, a Jacobite white rose pinned to his bonnet. He had just received a letter from his brother, Prince Henry Benedict, saying that the French would invade England on 9 December and, to his gratification, the people of Manchester were actually volunteering to enlist in his army. No fewer than 200 recruits presented themselves, and he formed them into the Manchester Regiment. When the wisdom of continuing was questioned yet again in his council that day, he simply told them about his brother's letter and they were suitably impressed. Lord George obligingly suggested that any discussion could be deferred until they reached Derby.

When they arrived in Macclesfield the next day, they learned that Cumberland was very near. He was believed to be at Stafford. Seriously concerned about being outnumbered, Lord George proposed leading his own column westwards in a feint towards Wales. The main army could then slip past the government troops and race ahead to

London. He therefore marched towards Congleton, and, sure enough, Cumberland followed him. The Duke drew up his army in battle order at Stone, and waited in vain for the Jacobites to appear. At last, some eight hours later, he realised that he had been duped. The Prince was on his way south still, and on the following day he entered Derby.

It was after dusk when he came in and as he looked around him he could see bonfires burning and celebratory candles flickering in windows. He took up residence in Exeter House and there he dined with his principal officers. Once again, the conversation turned to his favourite topic, the arrangements for his triumphal entry into London, and he scarcely paid any attention when Lord George rose abruptly to his feet and withdrew, saying that he had work to do. That night, his men seized Swarkeston Bridge, four miles south of the town. The road ahead was clear. Charles retired to bed happy in the knowledge that he was now nearer London than either Cumberland or Wade. Victory, he believed, was within his grasp.

Next morning he rose at his accustomed early hour and held a council of war in his lodgings, expecting to arrange the final details of the march on the capital. To his astonishment, Lord George opened the debate by announcing flatly that the time had come to turn back. They would not be able to capture London without defeating three armies. It was impossible. They would have to retire at once.

'To retire, Lord George? To retire?' cried the Prince, unable to believe his ears. 'Why, the clans kept me quite another language and assured me they were all ready to pierce [the enemy] or to die!'

Turning contemptuously from his troublesome Lieutenant-General, he addressed the other leaders, outlining his plans for their continued advance. He had uttered only a few sentences when Lord George interrupted him brusquely. It had not yet been decided whether they should advance at all, he snapped, and when the Prince looked round

the table he was aghast to find his other officers nodding their sombre
agreement.

One after another, the clan chiefs and the noblemen spoke, and each
of them urged a retreat. Stunned by their attitude, Charles exclaimed
that they were turning their backs on certain victory and on their
chance to restore the Stuart monarchy. Even that failed to move them.
As usual, they let Lord George speak for them and he summed up the
situation with his customary bluntness. They were all perfectly
prepared to die for the Stuart cause, he said, and that was precisely
what they would have to do if they went on. At that, there was a
chorus of agreement, some of those present adding placatingly that
they could not possibly risk their Prince's life by advancing.

With mounting agitation Charles argued, trying desperately to make
them change their minds. The Hanoverians were terrified of the
Jacobite army, he said. Ever since Prestonpans they had feared them.
London was in a panic and at this very moment his English supporters
were preparing to rise. They were only waiting for the French to
appear and that would happen almost immediately. Lord John
Drummond had told him so.

Where, said the council, was proof of the English Jacobites'
intentions? If Charles could show them letters promising their help,
they would go on. He could not. Contrary to what he had led them to
believe, he had not actually corresponded with the English Jacobites

107. Swarkeston Bridge,
just south of Derby, the
furthest point south
reached by the Prince's
army. Exeter House,
where he lodged in the
town, has long since been
demolished.
(© Great Scot! Pictures)

108. *William, Duke of Cumberland*, painted about 1748–9, by an artist of the school of D. Morier. (National Portrait Gallery, London)

and he had no written assurances from them. Even O'Sullivan refused to speak in his favour when that was revealed, and the Duke of Perth simply leaned his head wearily against the fireplace and listened in silence. Eventually, after more bitter exchanges, the meeting broke up in disorder.

Determined to get written assurances somehow or other, the Prince rode desperately round the neighbourhood to speak to probable supporters, but not one of the gentlemen he saw would do anything as incriminating as express loyalty to the Stuarts in writing. Back he went to Derby. Surely he could persuade some of the council to support him? The Duke of Perth usually upheld his views and the Marquis of Tullibardine had not been at the morning meeting. Out of personal respect for him, these two did agree to speak on his behalf when the council reassembled. So did O'Sullivan and Murray of Broughton, who was not a council member, but they made it plain that they had serious reservations.

All too soon, evening came and the council met again in Exeter House. Lord George spoke first, and it was as if the retreat had already been agreed. If they set out at once, he said calmly, they would have two days' start on Cumberland. They would go back the way they had come, lodging in the same quarters, and the cannon must be sent well ahead so as not to delay them. If they proceeded thus, he guaranteed that he would get them all safely back to Scotland.

As the Prince listened, he grew more and more distraught. Going back would be fatal, he cried. They would be caught between Cumberland and Wade, the very danger they had managed to avoid on their way south. Although the Duke of Perth did murmur a few words of agreement, no one else paid any attention. Cameron of Lochiel spoke in favour of Lord George's proposal that they should set out right away, whereupon Charles exclaimed in despair, 'You ruin, abandon and betray me if you do not march on!', but they simply looked at him in silence. As he himself admitted long afterwards he 'could not prevail upon one single person to support him'. He, the Prince, had been overruled. In the end he was forced to consent to the retreat, saying bitterly, 'In future I shall summon no more councils since I am accountable to nobody for my actions but to God and my father, and therefore I shall no longer either ask or accept advice'. With that, he quit the chamber.

A reception for the local Jacobites had been arranged for that evening and it was too late to cancel it. The Prince was forced to attend as if nothing had happened. As he strove to conceal his feelings, his jostling guests upset a table which fell against the Royal Standard, breaking it in two. Those who had been in the council that day looked at each other significantly.

Before dawn the next morning, they began to move out. It was 6 December, 'Black Friday', as the Jacobites would call it ever after. It was still dark, of course, and most of the clansmen did not realise that they had changed direction. Like the Prince, they had been elated at the thought of London and they could not wait to get there. As dawn came, however, and they began to recognise the familiar landmarks they had so recently passed, there were loud cries of dismay and anger, while the highland ladies in their coaches wept copious tears.

Not until nine o'clock that morning did the Prince mount his bay horse to ride after them in a mood of savage despair. According to his servant John Hay, 'Charles, who had marched a-foot at the head of the men all the way, was obliged to get on horseback, for he could not walk and hardly stand (as was always the case with him when he was cruelly used)'. The Prince was heard to say that he 'wished he had been twenty feet underground rather than see this day'.

109. King's colour of Barrell's Regiment, part of the government force. This colour was later carried at Culloden.
(On loan to the Scottish United Services Museum from The Stewart Society)

Hay was not an entirely reliable witness and his description may contain an element of exaggeration, but there is no doubt that the Prince was feeling utterly demoralised. Not only had all his hopes been brutally snatched away on the very verge of triumph but he had suffered an unbearable personal humiliation. His right to rule had been called into question, his decision reversed, and all this had taken place in the full view of the rest of Europe. Soon they would all know: George II, Louis XV and, worst of all, his own father. Always subject to bouts of depression, he was plunged into the most profound melancholy.

Each day the army set out early in its desperate race for the north. Once they got to Preston, said Lord George, they would be safe, but for the Prince each mile further away from London brought mortification and dismay. He rose late, infuriating Lord George by the delay, and then he rode grimly past his men to the next stopping place. The weather was bitterly cold, snow and ice making the going treacherous, and there were no bonfires and candles now but a population which was openly hostile. People jeered and threw stones. Some of the militia even risked firing at what they believed to be a vanquished army.

Back they went, through Ashbourne and Leek to Manchester. 'It is all over now: we shall never come back again', said the usually ebullient Colonel O'Sullivan, but Charles was not willing to give up so easily. Ever volatile, he was recovering from the dreadful reverse at Derby. He had persuaded himself that this was not a retreat, merely a strategic withdrawal. He knew that the French really were assembling their force of 12,000 men in the Channel ports and that knowledge gave him confidence. He reached the conclusion that once Lord John

110. A soldier of Lord Sempill's Regiment of Foot, part of the government force. (Army 1742 Clothing Book, National Museums of Scotland)

111. 'The Rebel Tree' at
Clifton, marking the scene
of the skirmish.
(© Great Scot! Pictures)

Drummond came south with his men the English Jacobites would act at last. This was merely an interlude, tiresome but far from fatal to his plans.

Lord George was still insisting on setting a rapid pace for the border, but each time they paused for the night, the Prince argued for a longer halt. It was 'a shame for to go so fast before the son of the Usurper', he told his Irish friends over supper in Lancaster, and there was nothing he would have liked better than to stop and face Cumberland.

In spite of being delayed by the weather, the fatigue of his men and the arrival of conflicting messages from London about the French invasion, Cumberland was not far behind. Indeed, an advance troop of his cavalry managed to attack the Jacobite rearguard as they laboured up the hills of Cumbria, but Lord George beat them off near Clifton.

This minor victory delighted the Prince and by the time he arrived in Carlisle on 19 December he felt able to ride proudly at the head of his army, followed by his now somewhat dishevelled Lifeguards. He found letters waiting for him in the city, from both France and Scotland. The French dispatches brought heartening news of the invasion preparations and from Scotland Lord John Drummond spoke of the men and money he was collecting. He did not explain why he had so far failed to move south, but the Prince assumed that he was on the point of leaving at last.

Charles was convinced that he would meet these welcome reinforcements within a few miles of Carlisle, whereupon they would turn

112. The Prince's money box.
(In the collection of the Duke of Buccleuch and Queensberry, KT, at Drumlanrig)

113. The Prince's camp kettle.
(In the collection of the Duke of Buccleuch and Queensberry, KT, at Drumlanrig)

south together. He therefore insisted on leaving a garrison in the castle, against all the advice of Lord George Murray. Cumberland would be able to capture it with no trouble at all, Lord George said, for he could easily bring guns from elsewhere and the defences were so poor that those within the castle would be unable to save themselves. The Prince would not listen. The Manchester Regiment, unwilling to enter Scotland, volunteered to act as part of the garrison and it was agreed to leave over 400 men there in all, two-thirds of them Scots, the rest English, with a handful of French.

Late on the morning of 20 December the Jacobites left Carlisle. They reached the border that afternoon. The River Esk was no longer a shallow, easily crossed stream. Swollen with snow and rain, it had become a deep and dangerous torrent. After anxious consultations, the Prince and his cavalry rode in to form a chain across the swift-flowing river. The clansmen then linked arms and crossed, ten or twelve abreast, some twenty-five yards away from them. Only their heads and shoulders could be seen above the water and some were almost swept away. However, the Duke of Perth and the other horsemen rode hastily to the rescue and the Prince himself saved one young Macdonald by snatching him from the strong current that was whirling him downstream. In the end, all the soldiers crossed safely, but two of the women camp-followers were drowned.

It was growing dark when the last men clambered gladly up the bank. They lit bonfires to dry themselves off and when the pipers began to play they danced joyous reels, because they had a double cause for celebration. It was the Prince's twenty-fifth birthday, and they were safely back in Scotland at last.

7

FALKIRK AND CULLODEN

IN A mood of optimism, they left for Dumfries that same night. The Prince slept in Drumlanrig Castle, where some of his more enthusiastic followers slashed a portrait of William of Orange. At Douglas Castle, the Duke of Douglas at first refused to open his gates, but when he saw the cannon the Jacobites had with them he changed his mind. On 24 December they reached Hamilton and Charles spent Christmas in the palace there. The Duke of Hamilton was away from home, so he was able to enjoy shooting in the famous deerparks in suddenly pleasant weather. He had lost none of his old skill, he found, and one admiring member of his suite noted that he killed, or at least hit, everything at which he took aim. 'Without flattery, he was looked upon to be the best marksman in the army.'

This interlude for recreation was brief, however. Glasgow lay a few miles to the west and the soldiers were all for sacking it to punish the inhabitants for their former lack of co-operation. Lochiel hastened to dissuade them. The city was prosperous, thriving from the new tobacco trade with America, and it could provide not only money but much-needed supplies of food and clothing.

On 26 December 1745 the Prince marched in on foot at the head of the clans and took up residence in Shawfield House, a handsome mansion in the Trongate. There he held court, much as he had done at Holyrood. His retinue noticed that he took great pains with his

114. Glasgow in the eighteenth century. (Photograph of an engraving, *Scotland's Story*)

115. Medal
commemorating the
government recapture of
Carlisle.
(National Museums of
Scotland)

116. *Lord John Drummond,*
the Duke of Perth's
brother, painted in Rome
in 1739 by D. Dupra.
(Scottish National Portrait
Gallery)

appearance, wearing his most elegant French clothes. Each evening
crowds of local people came to watch him sup, and the ladies vied with
each other for the honour of serving him. It was as if the clock had
been put back, almost as if the humiliation at Derby had never taken
place.

He even decided to hold a review of his entire army. It no longer
mattered to him that his numbers were depleted, for Lord John
Drummond's arrival was imminent and his force would double the
total. The Jacobites therefore marched out proudly to Glasgow Green,
drums beating, bagpipes playing and colours flying. The Prince
inspected them and discovered with delight that remarkably few had
been lost from either sickness or desertion. So excellent had been the
discipline that his little force had marched into England, challenged
three armies and emerged again unscathed.

The satisfaction he derived from this discovery was soon dispelled,
however. No sooner had the review ended than exhausted messengers

arrived from Carlisle with the very news Lord George had feared. Cumberland had arrived outside the city, dismissed the castle as 'an old hen coop', sent for his guns and captured it. Many of the garrison had been killed and those officers who had survived were now awaiting trial for treason. Inevitably, they would be found guilty and executed.

Although he was not prepared to admit that he had miscalculated, the Prince was genuinely horrified at the reports of the carnage, and so he was all the more impatient to gather together his complete army. He knew that Lord John Drummond was coming at last, proceeding as quickly as he could with his disorganised force of squabbling highlanders, lowlanders, Irish and French, and dragging the heavy cannon he had brought to Scotland with him. Charles decided to set out to meet him and on 3 January he moved from Glasgow to Bannockburn House, near Stirling.

This large mansion was the home of Sir Hugh Paterson, an ardent Jacobite. Sir Hugh had good-naturedly brought up his ten nieces when they lost their father and the youngest was now installed at Bannockburn to act as his hostess for the Prince. Clementina Walkinshaw was named after her godmother, none other than Clementina Sobieska. She was a year older than Charles, attractive and sophisticated. Her sister was lady-in-waiting to the Hanoverian Princess of Wales and she had spent some years with her in London. She had all the courtly graces the Prince expected in a woman, and in addition there was the intriguing link with his own family. Her father, a diplomat, had known Charles's parents in Rome, hence his youngest daughter's name.

117. Bannockburn House, where Charles and Clementina Walkinshaw stayed in January 1746. Unfortunately there is no authentic portrait of Clementina.
(© Great Scot! Pictures)

According to Lord Elcho, Miss Walkinshaw became the Prince's mistress almost immediately. Some historians have questioned this in the light of Charles's apparent indifference to women, but the most recent research has shown that his lovelife was not as arid as was once supposed. Indeed, it seems rather that he was naturally monogamous in a notoriously promiscuous age. At any rate, Clementina herself was later to claim that her reputation was ruined that year and it seems significant that although her suitors before then had included no less a man than the Duke of Argyll, her marriage prospects abruptly fell away and no husband was forthcoming. Lord Elcho seems to have been right.

Whatever the developments in his personal life, Charles's military prospects seemed to be improving. Lord John Drummond appeared at last, bringing the numbers in the Jacobite army to a record 9000.

Moreover, he discoursed encouragingly about the coming French invasion of England. Ironically, even as he spoke, the French ministers were hearing for the first time about the retreat from Derby and their former desire to place a Stuart on the throne of Britain vanished instantly. After a very brief discussion, they cancelled all their plans. No fleet would set sail for England that year.

Charles, of course, had no inkling of these developments. He decided to put Scotland in order and then to set off for London once more. Sending a contingent of men to besiege the government garrison in Stirling Castle, he turned his own attention to Edinburgh. In his absence, the capital had reverted to its customary Hanoverian allegiance and battalions of British soldiers were reportedly arriving there in large numbers.

Wade had finally succeeded in giving up his command and his place had been taken by General Henry Hawley. A veteran of such military triumphs as Dettingen, Hawley was in his mid-sixties, with a daunting reputation for severity towards not only the enemy but his own troops. Known to them as 'Hangman Hawley', he erected a gallows wherever he went as a sign to his soldiers that military discipline would be strictly enforced. When the Prince heard of his arrival in Edinburgh, he knew that an engagement with the enemy was very near.

True to his vow at Derby, Charles had not called any council of war since the start of the retreat and instead it seemed to the resentful Scots that he was relying more than ever on the advice of Sir Thomas Sheridan and Colonel O'Sullivan. With a battle imminent, Lord George could bear it no longer and he sat down to write Charles one of his forthright letters, telling him that in future he must take the advice of his council.

'All operations for the carrying on of the war should be agreed on by the majority of those in His Royal Highness's presence', he declared, nor should any decision be reversed without consultation. Moreover, on the battlefield, the generals must have the power to take such emergency measures as they deemed necessary. Past experience had shown how vital such arrangements were, for 'had not a council determined a retreat from Derby, what a catastrophe must have followed in two or three days!' The army was, after all, 'an army of volunteers, and not mercenaries, many of them being resolved not to continue in the army were affairs settled'.

When this less than tactful missive was delivered to the Prince, he was lying in bed at Bannockburn House, suffering from a cold and a fever. Seeing the familiar writing of his Lieutenant-General on the packet, he unfolded it, read it and leaped out of bed in a fury. Lord George's comments were perfectly justified, even if they could have been worded more diplomatically, but Charles took them as a direct challenge to his authority. Seizing a pen, he composed a hasty reply.

'When I came to Scotland', he wrote, 'I knew well enough what I was to expect from my enemies, but I little foresaw what I meet with from my friends!' He and he alone had the King's authority to

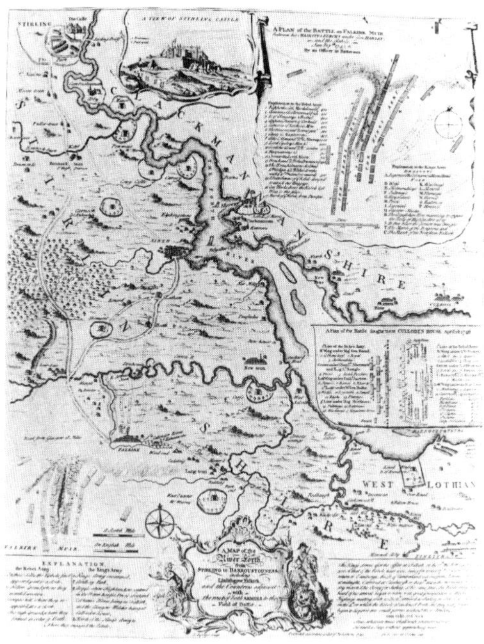

120. Map of the valley of
the River Forth, with a
plan of the Battle of Falkirk
inset.
(National Library of
Scotland)

command the army, he went on, and he particularly objected to the
sententious remarks about not treating the soldiers as mercenaries. 'I
am often hit in the teeth that this is an army of volunteers', he said,
'consisting of gentlemen of rank and fortune, and who came into it
merely upon motives of duty and honour. What one would expect
from such an army is more zeal, more resolution and more good
manners than in those that fight merely for pay, but it can be no army
at all where there is no general or, which is the same thing, no
obedience or deference paid to him.'

The chiefs might have much to lose, but he had even more. He had a
price on his head 'and therefore *I* cannot indeed threaten at every
other word to throw down my arms and make peace with the
government' and he ended with a final angry warning: 'My authority
may be taken from me by violence, but I shall never resign it like an
idiot!' It took all Clementina's powers of persuasion to calm him down
and get him back to bed again to continue his convalescence.

A week after this latest disagreement, General Hawley left Edinburgh
and made camp at Falkirk. Leaving the Duke of Perth with 1000 men to
continue the siege of Stirling Castle, the Prince marched to meet the
government army. He drew up his men on a hill to the west of Falkirk.
In front of the first line stood Lord George Murray, targe on arm,
sword in hand. Behind the second line was the Prince, on horseback,
with a small group of cavalry which would act as a reserve.

Thanks to the rapidity of their march, they were able to watch
Hawley's troops still assembling below them: a long line of horse,
followed by two lines of infantry. Even before the redcoats were all in
position, Hawley gave the order to attack. Until then the weather had

been unseasonably fine for 17 January, but now it grew very dark. It was almost as if there had been an eclipse, said one Jacobite officer afterwards. The wind rose and a squall of rain and hail half-hid the advancing enemy, he remembered, but when he did see 'this moving cloud of horse, regularly disciplined, in full trot upon us', he thought that his last hour had come.

He had reckoned without Lord George's skill as a general, however. Somehow, he made his excited men hold their ground, down on one knee, their muskets at the ready. Not until the dragoons were ten or twelve paces away did he give the order to fire. At the same moment, the wind veered, driving the icy rain straight into the faces of his adversaries.

When the Jacobites opened fire the government dragoons, cursing loudly, wheeled round and fled through their own ranks. Ignoring Lord George's orders, the Macdonalds set off in pursuit, but the rest of the clansmen stayed where they were, slashing with their swords at successive waves of footsoldiers until both government lines fell back in disarray. Within twenty minutes, the Prince's army was victorious.

The moment of triumph was marred, however, by total confusion about what was happening. Hearing more firing, the Macdonalds had turned back, and when the rest of the Jacobites saw them coming they thought they were being defeated. As a result, many of the second line began to flee from the battlefield, 'different clans mingled pell-mell together'. Charles himself rode over to try to restore order, but although he managed to drive back a small group of Hawley's dragoons, it was beyond anyone to rally the highlanders into any semblance of their battle lines.

To compound the confusion, when the Prince's officers looked over towards the enemy camp, they saw fires burning and they concluded that the General was still there, waiting to attack again. In fact, he was retreating towards Linlithgow. He had given orders that his tents should be burned, but the pouring rain soon quenched the flames, leaving his ammunition, baggage and provisions for the highlanders to find.

In spite of the appalling conditions, Charles remained on the battlefield until almost eight o'clock that night. He then rode to Falkirk, took possession of Hawley's quarters and ate the supper which had been prepared for the General. Meanwhile, Hawley had arrived safely back in Edinburgh and was applying himself to the unpleasant task of reporting his defeat to the Duke of Cumberland.

'Sir,' he wrote, 'My heart is broke . . . . We had enough to beat them, for we had 2000 men more than they. But such scandalous cowardice [on the part of his own soldiers] I never saw before. The whole second line of Foot ran away.' However, he promised that 'thirty-one of Hamilton's Dragoons are to be hanged for deserting to the rebels and thirty-two of the Foot to be shot for cowardice'.

The following day dawned just as wet. Once more, the rain poured down and, much as the Jacobites would have liked to pursue the enemy, it simply was not possible. The Prince rode back to the

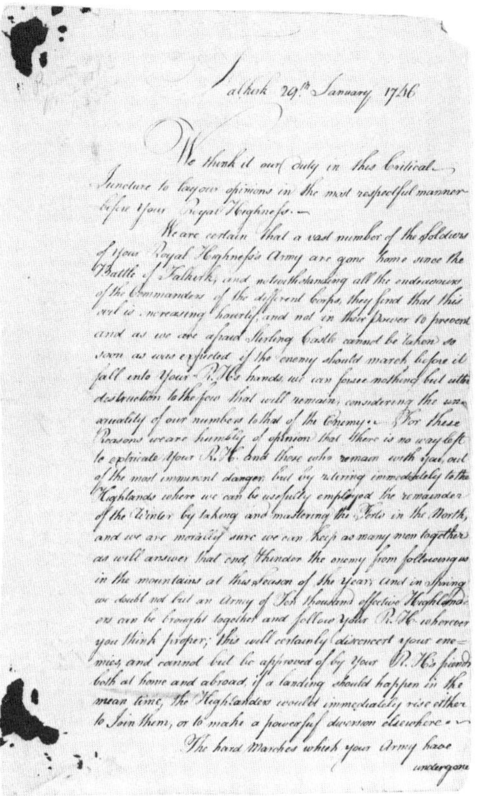

121. Address by the clan
chiefs at Falkirk,
requesting Charles to
retire to the highlands.
(Scottish Record Office)

battlefield to supervise the burial of the dead: 400 government soldiers and almost fifty of his own men. His officers stayed in Falkirk, quarrelling bitterly, blaming each other for the chaos on the battlefield and the escape of Hawley and the survivors.

With so many of the highlanders having fled home, it was hard to see any real long-term benefit accruing from the battle, and the Prince wrote to tell Louis XV, 'This victory removes my difficulties for the present, but Your Majesty will recognise that the contest will be very unequal if I do not receive much more help soon'.

He could do nothing constructive until the vanishing clansmen returned, and so he went back to Bannockburn House to keep in close touch with the siege of Stirling Castle. There was little sign of progress there, for the engineer in charge was disastrously incompetent, but when he heard that the Duke of Cumberland was on his way north to take over from Hawley, Charles at once felt more cheerful. Always happy at the prospect of positive action, he put aside his fears of being outnumbered and asked Lord George to draw up a battle plan. Lord George obliged and they spent an unusually harmonious evening going over it together. The Prince approved the plan, apart from a few 'corrections' which he inserted with his own hand, and he sat up late discussing the coming encounter in a state of high good humour.

He was all the more affronted when he rose rather late the following

morning to find waiting for him a letter signed by Lord George and the clan chiefs: a letter with an unmistakable message.

'We are certain that a vast number of the soldiers of Your Royal Highness's army are gone home since the battle of Falkirk', it said, 'and as we are afraid Stirling Castle cannot be taken so soon as expected, if the enemy should march before it fall into Your Royal Highness's hands we can foresee nothing but utter destruction.' They believed that 'there is no way to extricate Your Royal Highness and those who remain with you out of the most imminent danger but by retiring immediately to the Highlands'. They could come south again in the spring.

John Hay, the Prince's servant, was now acting as his secretary, and he reported that when Charles read the letter, 'he struck his head against the wall until he staggered, and exclaimed most violently against Lord George Murray. His words were, "Good God! Have I lived to see this?" ' As he demanded in his reply, 'Is it possible that a victory and a defeat should produce the same effect and that we conquerors should fly from an engagement while the conquered are seeking it?'

He could hardly believe that the situation at Derby was being repeated. 'I can't see nothing but ruin and destruction to us all in case we should think of a retreat', he told the chiefs, but try as he might he could not persuade them to change their minds and in the end he was forced to accept their decision.

'After all this', he said bitterly, 'I know I have an army that I cannot command any further than the chief officers please, and therefore if you are all resolved upon it I must yield, but I take God to witness that it is with the greatest reluctance and that I wash my hands of the fatal consequences which I foresee but cannot help.'

That same day his guns opened fire on Stirling Castle but they had been set at the wrong angle. The cannonballs soared uselessly overhead, the garrison fired back and the Jacobite gun emplacements were demolished. When thirty of the Prince's army lay dead and a further fifty had been wounded, the siege was abandoned. Morale sank lower than ever, and it was in an atmosphere of recrimination and despair that they set out for the highlands.

Amidst snow and rain, they marched north through Perthshire to Crieff, Castle Menzies and then Blair Atholl. The Duke of Cumberland had by now arrived in Edinburgh and he set off in pursuit. He realised, however, that if the Jacobites sought refuge in the remote glens he would be unable to follow them. He therefore decided to wait in Aberdeen, poised for an attack as soon as spring came.

The Prince's army scattered, some setting off to harry Lord Loudon's government force in the north, others to attack enemy posts elsewhere and Lord George to besiege his own ancestral home, for Blair Castle had fallen into the hands of the Hanoverians. After a short stay at Moy Hall with the redoubtable Lady MacIntosh, the Prince installed himself first at Lord President Forbes's mansion at Culloden, then in the house of Lady MacIntosh's mother-in-law in Inverness. During a brief visit to Elgin, he suffered an alarming illness, a violent fever which his anxious gentlemen feared might turn into pneumonia. He was forced to take to his bed for more than a week, but once he had been bled he felt better. In spite of the fact that he still had a temperature he ignored his doctor's orders, got up and declared that 'people were sick only when they thought themselves so'.

Still pretty low, he went back to Inverness, where he was greeted with some encouraging news. A Spanish ship had arrived at Barra bearing £4000 and 2500 stands of arms. The effect of this was rather spoiled, unfortunately, when the British captured the sloop *The Prince Charles*, which had been bringing men, stores and £12,000 for him from France. However, at least it showed that the French had not abandoned his cause as so many people now alleged.

It was proving increasingly difficult to raise the spirits of his men. Both food and money were in short supply, and everyone was conscious of Cumberland's threatening presence on the east coast. The Prince himself was becoming more and more perturbed about Lord George Murray, who was taking a suspiciously long time to capture Blair Castle. Could it be, suggested O'Sullivan, that because it was his

123. Charles's travelling
medicine chest, containing
158 different medical
preparations, including
remedies for toothache,
fevers and dyspepsia. Sir
Stuart Threipland had
charge of it.
(On loan to the National
Museums of Scotland from
the Royal College of
Physicians, Edinburgh)

124. *Sir Stuart Threipland,*
the Prince's chief
physician during the later
part of the campaign. He
commissioned this portrait
by W. Delacour to mark
his narrow escape from
death after Culloden.
(Mr & Mrs Mark Murray
Threipland)

brother's house, he was not really trying? When he finally abandoned
the attempt and rode to join the others, Lord George met with a chilly
reception.

During this uneasy interlude the Prince worked hard to improve the
morale of his troops, keeping up a deliberately cheerful front whatever
his own doubts. He went out shooting, gave balls and even danced at
them himself. He would hear no talk of failure and he often told

125. *Major Hugh Fraser*,
one of the Scottish officers
in the government army,
by an unknown artist.
(National Museums of
Scotland)

people that he would go on fighting even if he had only two men left. This was no idle boast. He meant it.

Slowly, time passed. As March drew to a close, the cold spring winds dried up the ground, the rivers fell and the Duke of Cumberland prepared to advance. The Prince sent orders to his scattered followers to join him at Inverness and spoke of marching to Aberdeen to attack the enemy in their camp. Before he could gather enough men to do so, Cumberland marched to Cullen, crossed the River Spey, reached Elgin and halted at the small village of Alves. A fleet of transport vessels was sailing alongside, close to the coast, with plentiful supplies of food and ammunition for him.

On 14 April 1746 he reached Nairn and the Prince marched out of Inverness. He and his officers took up their quarters in Culloden House while their men lay down to rest among the trees and furze of Culloden Wood. Next morning, he sent Colonel O'Sullivan out to select a battlefield. His commanders were urging him to wait for the rest of his army to assemble, but he brushed them aside impatiently and on the Colonel's advice he gave orders that the men were to be drawn up on Culloden Moor, a stretch of the larger Drummossie Moor, about a mile and a half south-east of Culloden House.

When he rode over to review his army, he discovered that they were desperately hungry. Many of them had not eaten for hours and so he sent to Inverness for supplies. Unfortunately, all he could get was one biscuit for each person. As soon as the review was over, Lord George engaged him in a heated argument about the choice of battlefield, but the Prince would not hear of any alternative. By this time it was early afternoon. There was still no sign of the enemy and all was reported to be quiet in their camp. Someone remembered that it was Cumberland's twenty-fifth birthday. Presumably he and his men would spend the

126. Culloden House, home of Lord President Forbes, occupied by Charles in the spring of 1746.
(Photograph, Royal Commission on Ancient Monuments, Scotland)

127. Lord President Forbes's bedchamber at Culloden House, used by the Prince during his stay.
(Culloden House sale catalogue 1897: photograph, Royal Commission on Ancient Monuments, Scotland)

day celebrating. The Prince ordered his own soldiers back to their quarters.

A few hours later he called his officers to a council and in the course of their discussions Lord George came up with an exciting new scheme. Saying that it was dangerous for them to wait to be attacked, outnumbered as they were, he suggested that instead they should fall upon the enemy camp by night. After a day's carousing, Cumberland and his redcoats would be in no fit state to defend themselves and the Jacobites could inflict a crushing defeat. Charles was delighted with the idea. There was an irritating delay while they fetched back the men who had gone off to Inverness again to look for food but by eight o'clock that evening they were ready to move off. The Prince embraced Lord George, who placed himself at the head of the first column and set out with his customary alacrity. The Prince rode some way behind, with the second column coming after him.

So convinced was he that victory was within his reach that Charles was ready to set aside all his previous differences with his Lieutenant-General. They had not gone very far when he rode up to Lord George, dismounted and threw a friendly arm round his shoulders.

'Lord George!' he cried, 'You can't imagine, nor I can't express to you, how acknowledging I am of all the services you have rendered me, but this will crown all. You'll restore the King by it, you'll deliver our poor country from slavery. . . . Be assured, dear Lord George, that the King and I will never forget it!' Lord George remained grimly silent. He merely removed his bonnet and bowed stiffly. He did not forget past insults so easily.

Apart from that, he was assailed by the gravest doubts about the whole expedition. They had been far too late in leaving, the ground was marshy, it was pitch dark and the men were so tired and hungry that many of them felt lightheaded and faint. They could not keep up their normal speed and the second column was continually sending up messages begging him to slow down. Lord George complied, but he was growing increasingly irritable.

When they reached the banks of the River Nairn he halted. Lochiel came riding up and they agreed that they would never reach Nairn before dawn. The plan had failed. There was no alternative but to retreat. Furious at the collapse of his scheme, Lord George turned abruptly about and set off back the way he had come.

Knowing nothing of all this, the Prince was astonished when he saw the first column returning towards him. 'Where the devil are the men a-going?' he demanded, and when he realised that they were retreating he called out, 'I am betrayed! What need I give orders when my orders are disobeyed?'

It fell to the Duke of Perth to explain and he managed to placate Charles by reminding him that they could yet confront Cumberland on the battlefield. 'Tis no matter then', the Prince declared, 'we shall meet them and behave like brave fellows.'

It did matter, of course, and that abortive night march had a critical effect on what was to follow. By the time the Jacobites arrived back at Culloden it was nearly six in the morning and they were utterly exhausted. 'Everybody seemed to think of nothing but sleep', said Lord Elcho, and he described in his memoirs how the Prince and his officers were too weary to contemplate a council of war. Instead, 'everyone laid himself down where he could, some on beds, others on tables, chairs and on the floors'. The ordinary soldiers flung themselves down on the heathery ground in the park.

Just two hours later, one of the Camerons was hammering on the doors of Culloden House with urgent news. Cumberland's army had been sighted. The Prince, Lord George and the others rose hastily, ran out of the house and mounted their horses. The drums beat and the

128. View of Culloden
Moor.
(National Trust for
Scotland)

pipes played to summon the men. Their sound 'caused great hurry and confusion amongst people half dead with fatigue' and some of the soldiers were so tired that they did not wake at all, until it was too late. Others were back in Inverness and whole regiments still had not arrived. The Marquis d'Eguilles pleaded with the Prince to retreat but he could not. With no provisions, that was out of the question. They would have to fight.

Fewer than 5000 men responded to the pipes and drums. They marched up to Culloden Moor again, where a fierce argument broke out between the Macdonalds and Lord George about who should have the place of honour on the right. Lord George was determined that it should go to his Atholl men and he would not budge. Eventually, the Prince had to exercise all his powers of persuasion to convince the Macdonalds that they must go to the left. While they took up their positions in surly silence, Charles rode up and down the lines, shouting encouragingly, 'Here they are coming, my lads! We'll soon be with them!' He then went to his own place on a slope behind the second line. From that vantage point he would command his army. With him went a small group of reserve cavalry, and what remained of Lord Elcho's Lifeguards.

It was 16 April 1746, a dull, wet, misty day. A cold wind blew into the faces of the Jacobites. At about half past eleven they saw the redcoats coming towards them and they realised that they were vastly outnumbered. Cumberland had 2400 horse and 6400 foot. When he arrived within two and a half miles of the Prince's army he halted and put his troops into battle order. The two lines of foot, one behind the

other, were flanked by cavalry at either side. Thus deployed, they began to advance again. Five or six hundred paces from the Jacobites, they stopped to position their guns at intervals between their battalions. A great cheer went up from each side, the highlanders opened fire and Cumberland's gunners responded with devastating effect.

His cannon cut great swathes through the Jacobite ranks, soon putting the Prince's guns out of action and even killing one of the grooms standing near him on his little hill. The clansmen's natural instincts were to charge, but their chiefs held them back. They must allow the enemy to advance, as Hawley had done at Falkirk. Under the government army's merciless fire they waited, the snow and hail blowing into their faces, their friends and relatives falling dead and wounded around them.

Still Cumberland's men did not come forward. At last, the chiefs knew that they could hold the highlanders no longer. The Prince sent the order to charge, but his aide-de-camp, who was carrying the message to Lord George, was killed before he could deliver it. Another man was sent down but by the time he got through the Mackintoshes had already broken away, surging forward without even waiting to discharge their muskets.

As they charged on, the enemy guns fired grapeshot at them and they veered to the right, pressing Lord George and his right wing against a low stone wall at their side. On they all went, pushing and jostling, crushed together so tightly that they could scarcely draw their swords. Stumbling over the bodies of their own men, they forced their way ahead to find Cumberland's infantry bearing down on them. Many were killed by the musket fire of the government front line:

129. *A Jacobite Incident: Culloden*, painted by D. Morier, using Jacobite prisoners from the '45 as models for the highlanders.
(Reproduced by gracious permission of Her Majesty The Queen)

130. Coloured engraving of the Battle of Culloden.
(National Library of Scotland.)

144

s in *SCOTLAND*, 16th April 1746.

ee Lines, into the left of which the Rebels attempting to break with

ing, and the Dragoons the Rear, which compleated the Rout of the

the Pursuit and 1800 taken Prisoners.

Warehouse, N.º 69 in S.ᵗ Pauls Church Yard, LONDON.

131. Clan Cameron
banner, carried by
Lochiel's standard-bearer
at Culloden.
(Sir Donald Cameron of
Lochiel, KT)

others who did get through perished on the bayonets of the second line.

On the left wing, the Duke of Perth was frantically urging the Macdonalds to charge. Still furious at being displaced, they faltered when the order to advance was given. Seizing their standard, the Duke shouted that if they behaved with their usual valour they would make the left the new position of honour and he would ever afterwards take the name Macdonald for his own.

At that, Macdonald of Keppoch cried out in Gaelic, 'My God, have the children of my clan forsaken me?' and he dashed forward, his pistol in one hand, his drawn sword in the other. His men followed him then, but after a few yards he fell wounded. A friend helped him up and urged him to escape. 'Save yourself!' he replied, and staggered on to die under a hail of shot. As Cumberland's dragoons came thundering to the attack, the clansmen left the field, protected by the Irish contingent.

The Prince watched the slaughter from his position behind the second line. Some said later that he tried to go down to rally his men and had to be restrained from doing so. Others claimed that he gazed in horrified disbelief at the scene before him, too shocked to move. According to one account, Lord Elcho shouted at him that he was a 'damned cowardly Italian'. Whatever the truth of it, Sir Thomas Sheridan and Colonel O'Sullivan were determined that his life must be saved at all costs. One of them took his horse by the bridle and they led him from the field.

132. Book of Common
Prayer carried during the
campaign by William
Hynd, one of the English
soldiers in the government
army.
(National Museums of
Scotland)

146

133. Cairn erected on the battlefield in 1881, in memory of the fallen Jacobites.
(National Trust for Scotland)

134. Inscription on the cairn at Culloden.
(Photograph, National Museums of Scotland)

135. The Well of the Dead at Culloden.
(National Trust for Scotland)

8

THE FUGITIVE

GALLOPING desperately westwards, the Prince and his companions rode for the River Nairn. All around them was
confusion. On the moor, the air was filled with the groans of the
injured and the dying. Many Jacobites were fleeing frantically towards
Inverness, pursued by the government dragoons. Cumberland had
ordered them to give no quarter and so they killed the wounded and
those highlanders still slumbering in the park as well as the panic-
stricken combatants.

Arriving at the river, Charles crossed and halted on the other side,
about four miles from the battlefield. Those of his men who were
officially in the service of the French knew that they could safely give
themselves up. They were not subjects of George II and they would
suffer no reprisals. For the Prince, it was different. He was the
Pretender's son, the leader of this rising, and he had a price on his
head.

For that reason, Sir Thomas Sheridan and the others feared not only
the redcoats but the Scottish Jacobites. Charles had from childhood
heard the story of how the Scots handed over Charles I to the enemy
after his surrender to them during the Civil War and it seemed that he
might well suffer a similar fate. Apart from that, as a climax to all the
months of acrimony between the Prince and Lord George Murray,
Charles and his Irishmen had convinced themselves, quite unjustifi-
ably, that their general had betrayed them. The defeat was his fault,
they told each other, and it was no accident. He had deliberately
thrown away the chance of victory. Anxious to separate themselves as
quickly as possible from their Scottish companions, they ordered the
Lifeguards to seek shelter in the barracks at Ruthven, which were
being held for the Jacobites. Charles would set out in a different
direction, taking with him only Sir Thomas, Colonel O'Sullivan and a
handful of others.

Off they went, stopping briefly at a house where Lord Lovat was
staying. Perhaps he could offer some advice. A devious, wily old
schemer now in his late seventies, he had sent his clan to join the
Prince's cause after Prestonpans. Now he knelt before Charles, kissed
his hand and attempted to console him by observing that his great
ancestor, King Robert the Bruce, had suffered eleven defeats before
winning his final, overwhelming victory. The Prince must try again.
Sir Thomas and the Colonel were horrified at the suggestion. They
drew Charles to one side and begged him not to listen. It would be
folly to continue. He must flee to France.

None of the accounts of what happened during these confused
hours makes clear Charles's own attitude at that point. His enemies
would say afterwards that he was in a state of panic, self-preservation

136. Ruthven Barracks,
built for government
troops between 1719–21,
where some of the Jacobite
leaders assembled after
Culloden.
(In the care of Historic
Buildings and
Monuments, SDD, and
open to the public)

(Scottish Tourist Board)

137. Song celebrating Cumberland's victory at Culloden, with music by Handel.
(National Library of Scotland)

his only consideration. In fact the Prince was no coward and he did send a message to the clans urging them to rally to him at Fort Augustus, but when he got there himself he waited a mere two hours, far too little time to allow any of those on foot to reach him.

Meanwhile, those highlanders who were not fleeing to their homes were going to Ruthven, and as the evening passed their leaders staggered wearily into the barracks there: the Duke of Perth and his brother Lord John, Lord Ogilvy, the surviving clan chiefs and finally, dirty and dishevelled, his hat and wig lost, his coat cut and torn and his sword broken, Lord George Murray. Greeting each other emotionally, they settled down to await instructions from the Prince. Eventually, a message came: a message which was practical enough, but hardly the rousing call to arms they were expecting. They must do what was necessary to save themselves, the royal emissary told them.

Charles and his companions, half-dead with hunger and exhaustion, had by then left the fort and were riding another three miles to seek refuge in Glengarry Castle. To their horror, they found that it was deserted but at least it gave them shelter while they finalised their plans. The Prince would ride to Arisaig. Once more, it is difficult to discover his true motives. Some have claimed that his intention was to place himself at the head of his men and fight on if he encountered enough of them along the way. It is more probable, however, that his real aim was to find a ship sailing to France as soon as he could.

He would have to travel quickly and secretly, and the fewer people he took with him, the better. No longer would he have his valet, his physician, his barber, his cook and his admiring retinue. Even Sir Thomas would have to stay behind, for he was patently unfit for such an arduous journey. Colonel O'Sullivan, Alan Macdonald, the Prince's confessor, and Edward Burke, a guide, would be his only companions. For greater safety, Charles changed clothes with Burke and then they set off down the shores of Loch Lochy, along Loch Arkaig and so to Arisaig.

For almost a week the Prince stayed there in the cottage of Alexander Macdonald. During this time he was gradually joined by other survivors of the battle but they were far too few in number to make any new attempt possible. Lord George Murray himself knew that the situation was hopeless. 'Besides our defeat,' he said afterwards, 'there was neither money nor provisions to give, so no hope was left.' He wrote the Prince another of his letters, telling him he should never have raised the standard in the first instance without firm promises of support. That done, Lord George, Cameron of Lochiel, who had been wounded in both ankles, and the other Jacobite leaders dispersed to seek refuge throughout the highlands.

Escape to France now seemed the only possibility if Charles were to survive, and, fearing that Loudon's men from Skye were about to travel through Arisaig, he felt that he must move at once. No French vessel had yet managed to slip past the British men-of-war patrolling the west coast and so he decided to seek refuge with some of the Hanoverian chiefs, believing that they would not betray him. His horrified highlanders could not allow that and, much against their advice, he resolved that he would travel instead to the Outer Hebrides. While he waited for an old boat to be made ready, he composed a farewell letter to the chiefs.

'When I came into this country,' he wrote, 'it was my only view to do all in my power for your good and safety. This I will always do as long as life is in me. But alas! I see with grief that I can at present do little for you on this side of the water, for the only thing that can now be done is to defend yourselves till the French assist you.'

He was going back to get help, he said, but if for some reason Louis would not provide it, he would at least see that George II gave the Jacobites reasonable terms when they surrendered. In his absence, they should set up a council of all the chiefs and they could look for guidance to the Duke of Perth and Lord George Murray, he felt sure. They would 'stick by you to the very last'.

The letter written, he was ready to go. On 26 April, ten days after Culloden, he set sail from Loch nan Uamh, hoping to reach Eriskay, where he had first landed. No sooner had they left than a terrible storm blew up. The oarsmen were terrified, but the Prince stood shouting encouragement, and at about seven the next morning, after a

138. Benbecula, where Charles sought refuge after fleeing from the mainland. (Scottish Tourist Board)

dreadful voyage, they landed at Rossinish in Benbecula, further north than they had intended.

For two days they huddled in a miserable hut, sharing their meagre supply of water and oatmeal, while the storm raged around them. As soon as it cleared a little, they set out for Stornoway. There, the Prince hoped to hire a boat which would either take him direct to France or to Orkney, Norway and then south.

Ironically, even as he plodded onwards in pouring rain, two big French ships of war were sailing into Loch nan Uamh. Antoine Walsh, fearing the worst from the Scottish news, had sent them to rescue the Prince. They took aboard dozens of weary Jacobites including the Duke of Perth, Lord John Drummond, Lord Elcho and Sir Thomas Sheridan, but of Charles there was no sign. Next day, the vessels were attacked by a trio of British ships.

The French managed to drive them off, but they suffered serious damage as well as casualties and they knew that they could not risk a further attack by searching for Charles. Instead, they set sail for France. A few nights later, the Duke of Perth died, worn out by all his gallant efforts on the Prince's behalf. He was buried at sea. Before the voyage was completed, almost all the eighty-five men wounded in the seafight died too, and so did another sixty-seven when fever broke out on board one of the vessels.

139. Uist. For three weeks the Prince hid in a forester's hut at Coradale, in South Uist. (Photograph, National Museums of Scotland)

The Prince, of course, knew nothing of all this. He was wrestling with problems of his own. The people of Stornoway were so hostile that they would not even let him set foot in their town and they refused to hire him a boat. Seething with rage, he had to turn south again, seeking shelter in a series of wretched huts and bothies. His clothes were soaking, his shoes disintegrating, his feet bleeding and his limbs were numb with cold. Even so, he remained astonishingly cheerful. His companions never heard him complain and when they tried to sympathise with his discomfort he merely remarked that anything he had to endure was nothing compared with the sufferings of his army. So saying, he ate his oatmeal, using a shell as a spoon, supped his wretched gruel as if it were the most tasty dish concocted by his father's cooks in Rome and recoiled only when he had to drink from a dirty communal cup.

His patience and self-control amazed everyone, but Colonel O'Sullivan and the others were becoming increasingly worried about his health. He was painfully thin and pale and the Colonel at last discovered that he was suffering from dysentery. They plied him with brandy to settle his stomach and luckily they were able to find pleasanter quarters.

They had managed to contact Clanranald, who made available to them a forester's cottage at Coradale in South Uist. It was situated in a

140. Spoon end engraved with the initials CPR (Charles, Prince Regent) and the date, 3 July 1746. (Detail of 141). (National Museums of Scotland)

141. Silver knife, fork and spoon used by Charles during his period in hiding. He presented it to one of his helpers, Murdoch MacLeod, who later had the black shagreen case made. (National Museums of Scotland)

pretty valley and when he saw it the Prince declared that it looked like a palace compared with the abominable hut he had just left. His companions made him a seat out of green turf and he sat down to a meal of bread, cheese and goat's milk. When he had finished he asked them to bathe his lacerated feet. That done, he smoked a pipe of tobacco before lying down to sleep on a bed made out of heather and rushes.

He spent three weeks at Coradale, shooting, hunting and even dancing highland reels, whistling their tunes to himself. When his friends saw him one day sitting outside on a rock, his face turned up to the sun, they hurried over anxiously to warn him that he would get a headache, but he only laughed and said it was doing him good. To one who had been brought up in Italy, the sunshine was a welcome sight.

Clanranald not only provided him with shelter: he sent him food and fitted him out with a new highland outfit, complete with kilt and plaid. When he put on these garments he was, said Colonel O'Sullivan, 'quite another man'. Laughing merrily, the Prince leaped about and joked, 'I only want the itch to be a complete highlander!' Clanranald presented him with a silver drinking cup so that he would no longer have to endure the communal bowl and Lady Margaret Macdonald in Skye kept him supplied with newspapers.

Local Jacobite leaders visited him regularly, and he spoke with them long into the night. Sometimes he seemed depressed, but for the most part he talked cheerfully of his plans. The clansmen would be able to hold out until his return from France, he felt sure, and he often discussed his brother's impending arrival. Henry Benedict would invade England any day now, with his force of 12,000, he assured them. They did not have the heart to contradict him.

Not only did he and his visitors talk together. They drank together too and Neil MacEachain, who was now acting as their guide, spoke of seeing the Prince consume 'a whole bottle [of brandy] a day without

being in the least concerned'. He recalled one occasion when 'His Royal Highness was the only one who was able to take care of all the rest, heaping them with plaids and at the same time merrily sang the *De Profundis* for the rest of their souls'. Alcohol was becoming a defence against both physical discomfort and black despair.

This strange interlude could not be of long duration. Cumberland had realised that the Prince was no longer on the mainland and he knew that Cameron of Locheil and his friends were trying to raise support for the Stuart cause. He therefore harried the Jacobites unmercifully, burning their houses, terrorising their families and generally reinforcing his reputation as 'the Butcher', the name he had earned for himself at Culloden. Now he gave orders that the Outer Isles were to be thoroughly searched. As a result, frigates, sloops, bomb-ketches and cutters sailed up and down the coast, patrolling

142. *Admiral Thomas Smith*, commander-in-chief of British ships on the coasts of Scotland, engraved from a portrait by Richard Wilson.
(On loan to the Scottish National Portrait Gallery from the National Library of Scotland)

143. *Flora MacDonald,*
painted in London in 1747
by Richard Wilson. She
gave this portrait to the
captain of the ship which
took her south, in
gratitude for his kindness
to her.
(Scottish National Portrait
Gallery)

every bay and inlet. No one could travel in the islands without a passport and more and more soldiers were arriving to continue the search on land. Eventually, there were almost 2000 troops, mostly clansmen in government service, looking for the Prince.

It was no longer safe to linger near the shore. Instead, he would take to the mountains, but O'Sullivan, middle-aged, portly and tired out, would have to be left behind. The Colonel parted from him tearfully, promising to pass on word of the Prince's survival as soon as he got back to France for, said Charles, 'the greatest grief I had in my misery was the trouble I knew the King and the Duke were in about me'. O'Sullivan did get away soon afterwards, on a French cutter which had been vainly searching for the Prince.

Charles's guide, Neil MacEachain, was a tutor in Clanranald's family. He had been educated in France and spoke excellent French as well as Gaelic and English. He contacted the commander of the South Uist goverment militia. In spite of his position, Captain Hugh MacDonald was a staunch Jacobite and he always made sure that the Prince knew in advance exactly where his men would be searching.

Some years before, the Captain had married a widow with a young family. Their home was on Skye, but at present his stepdaughter was visiting her brother on South Uist. Miss Flora MacDonald, twenty-four years old, was slim, dark and dignified. She had been well brought-up, she was musical and she seemed intelligent, sensible and resourceful. Neil lost no time in approaching her with a plan. He would like her, he explained, to smuggle the Prince over to Skye, disguised as her maid.

Flora was horrified. Loyal as she was to the cause, she said straight out that such a scheme seemed to her 'both fantastical and dangerous'. She would have nothing to do with it. Neil was not so easily deterred, however, and he put another, less alarming proposal to her. Miss MacDonald could at least meet the Prince and talk with him, he suggested. Surely that would do no harm?

Flora's curiosity overcame her caution. She agreed and so it was arranged. Captain Felix O'Neill, an Irish soldier in French service had come over from the mainland with the Prince and his friends. He would bring Charles to her. At midnight she accordingly went to a lonely shieling belonging to her brother and there she met the Prince. One look at him was enough. Her heart melted. He was, she told people afterwards, 'in a bad state of health, of a thin and weak habit of body and greatly exhausted with fatigue and want of proper accommodation'. What impressed her most of all, though, was that 'under these calamities, he possessed a cheerfulness, magnanimity and fortitude remarkably great and incredible to all but such as saw him then'.

Telling him to stay hidden, she set off for Clanranald's house to make the necessary arrangements. On the way, a group of soldiers stopped her at one of the fords, demanding to see her passport. She did not have one and so they arrested her. She thereupon asked to speak to their commanding officer, knowing full well that he was her own stepfather.

When Captain MacDonald arrived the next day he ordered her immediate release and he also supplied her with a passport. It was

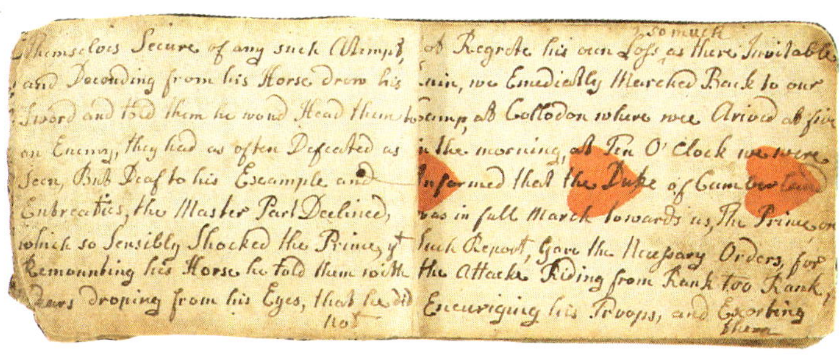

144. Diary kept on playing cards by Captain Felix O'Neill, who helped to arrange the Prince's escape to Skye.
(National Library of Scotland)

145. A snippet of the dress worn by Charles as 'Betty Burke', pasted into the inside cover of 'The Lyon in Mourning', a compilation of Jacobite recollections. Also preserved are a piece of 'Betty's' apron strings and a portion of the Prince's blue Garter ribbon. (National Library of Scotland)

made out to herself, her 'man-servant Neil MacEachain' and Betty Burke, 'an excellent spinner of flax and a faithful servant'. This mythical Irishwoman would really be the Prince, suitably disguised. Arriving at Clanranald's house, Flora quickly told Lady Clanranald of the plan and together they made some extra-large female clothing, collected provisions and hired a boat. All this took a week.

By 27 June, General Campbell and the government forces were closing in. The following evening, Flora and Lady Clanranald went down to the shore to meet the Prince and Captain O'Neill. They crouched down out of sight among the rocks and ate a hasty supper, but even as they did so an anxious servant came running down from Lady Clanranald's house. General Campbell had arrived at the door and was demanding to see her. Horrified, she hurried back to explain that she had been out visiting a sick child. The General questioned her closely, but she would not change her story and he left, apparently satisfied. A few days later, she and her husband were both arrested.

While Lady Clanranald was making her explanations to the General, Captain O'Neill was busy transforming the Prince into Betty Burke. Over his petticoat went a long, print dress and an apron. On his head was a frilled cap. His stockings were kept up by a pair of blue velvet French garters and his shoes were leather brogues. Thus arrayed, he showed himself off to Flora and Neil, who scrutinised him doubtfully. With his height and his regal bearing he did not make a convincing woman, but there was nothing they could do about it except beg him to shorten his stride and stop lifting his skirts so high when he walked.

Charles only laughed at these instructions. He was far more concerned about his lack of weapons. He wanted to conceal a pistol under his petticoat, but Flora would not hear of it. If he were searched,

she said reprovingly, the gun would be discovered and his secret would be out. He laughed even more at that, replying merrily, 'Indeed, Miss, if we shall happen to meet with any that will go so narrowly to work in searching as what you mean, they will certainly discover me at any rate!' He took her advice, though, and gave up the pistol although he did insist on carrying a stout stick which he could use as a cudgel.

They were ready to embark now, and together he, Flora and Neil climbed into a boat with four oarsmen. Captain O'Neill stayed behind. He tried to join the Prince in Skye a few days later, but before he could do so he was arrested and taken to England.

It was about nine in the evening when they set sail for Skye. The weather was very fine but they had not gone far when the seas grew rough and they ran into a storm. Nothing daunted, Charles kept up all their spirits by singing a selection of songs, notably his favourite, 'The

146. Charles in his 'Betty Burke' disguise, engraved by J. Williams.
(Scottish National Portrait Gallery)

147. Brogues worn by Charles as 'Betty Burke' and left by him with MacDonald of Kingsburgh.
(On loan to the National Museums of Scotland from Laurence Blair Oliphant of Ardblair)

King shall enjoy his own again'. Neil produced half a bottle of wine for him, but he insisted that it be kept for Flora. She might feel faint, he said, possibly remembering his own fragile mother. He insisted that she should lie down and rest in the bottom of the boat, and when she woke it was to find him guarding her carefully in case the oarsmen stepped on her by mistake.

Because they had no compass, they were uncertain where they were, but dawn revealed Waternish Point. Just as they were thinking of landing, soldiers appeared behind some rocks and began firing at them. They rowed away as fast as they could and hid in a creek. Eventually, they managed to go ashore twelve miles further north, at Trotternish. The militia were all around, and so the Prince stayed hidden while Flora and Neil went to see Lady Margaret Macdonald, the benefactor who had kept the Prince supplied with newspapers.

Although she had been warned the day before that the Prince was coming, Lady Margaret was appalled at her visitors' presence, for an officer of the government militia was in her house at that very moment. Luckily, her factor Alexander MacDonald of Kingsburgh was on hand and he agreed to take the Prince in. It was nearly eleven o'clock that night when the factor arrived home with his royal companion. His wife had already gone to bed, but her daughter rushed in to her chamber to tell her, 'Oh Mother! My father has brought in a very odd, ill-shaken up wife as ever I saw!'

Mrs MacDonald took this as a piece of girlish exaggeration but when she went downstairs she found 'such an odd, muckle trollop of a carlin [great, gangling woman] making long, wide steps through the hall' that she hardly knew what to think. Worse was to follow when the stranger kissed her politely and she felt the bristles on his chin. She hurried off to demand an explanation from her husband, but when she mentioned the bearded kiss he merely smiled calmly and said, 'Why, my dear, it is the Prince. You have the honour to have him in your house'.

'The Prince!' cried Mrs MacDonald, aghast, 'Oh Lord, we are all ruined and undone forever! We will all be hanged now!'

'Hoot, goodwife,' the factor retorted, 'we will die but once, and if we are hanged for this, I am sure we die in a good cause. Pray make no

148. The Prince's Bowl: a Chinese export porcelain bowl said to have been used by Charles at Kingsburgh House. (National Museums of Scotland)

delay. Go, get some supper. Fetch what is readiest. You have eggs and butter and cheese. . . .'

'Eggs and butter and cheese!' wailed his wife. 'What a supper is that for a Prince?'

'Oh, goodwife,' replied MacDonald, 'Little do you know how this good Prince has been living for some time past. These, I assure you will be a feast to him.'

The Prince did indeed enjoy his meal and afterwards he called for brandy and tobacco. 'I have learned in my skulking to take a hearty dram!' he exclaimed, drinking their healths and when they showed him to his chamber he threw himself down gladly on the comfortable bed and slept so late that Flora grew anxious about the delay. She sent the factor to rouse him and then she and Mrs MacDonald helped him into his Betty Burke clothes, a performance which had him 'like to fall over with laughing'.

'Oh, Miss,' he called out in an absurd voice, 'You have forgot my apron! Where is my apron? Pray get my apron here, for that is a principal part of my dress!'

Flora's repressive replies made him tease her all the more, and Mr MacDonald and his wife agreed that he behaved 'not like one that was in danger, but as cheerfully and merrily as if he had been putting on women's clothes merely for a piece of diversion'. They were entirely charmed with him and they found him so easy to speak to that Mr MacDonald even ventured to ask him if Lord George Murray was a traitor, as some people said. The Prince replied diplomatically that he would never allow any treachery or villainy to be laid at Lord George's door, although he did admit that 'he had much to bear of him from his temper'.

The day was well advanced before he was ready to go, but at last he said goodbye to the factor and his wife and they set off for Portree, Flora riding by one route, the Prince and Neil travelling on foot by another. As soon as he could, Charles discarded his Betty Burke outfit and, in highland dress once more, trudged through the rain. They met Flora at a Portree inn for a meal, and then they parted from her. The Prince was careful to pay her back a half crown he had borrowed from her, and when he left her he said as he always did on such occasions, 'I hope we shall meet in St James's yet, and I will reward you for what you have done'.

While he set sail for the little island of Raasay, she went home to her mother. She did not breathe a word of her adventure until more than a week later, when she was summoned by the militia, arrested and eventually taken to London where she was kept in the same house as Clanranald and his wife, the Prince's wigmaker, a man who had brought brandy to Charles at Coradale and various other Jacobites who had helped him. Another fellow-prisoner was Captain Felix O'Neill. He feared she might be angry, but when they met she slapped him lightly on the cheek, saying with a whimsical smile, 'To that black face do I owe all my misfortune!' They were released the following year when a general amnesty was declared.

149. Dunstaffnage Castle, where Flora was held briefly after her arrest. (In the care of Historic Buildings and Monuments, SDD, and open to the public)

That all lay in the future, however. For the moment, the Prince hid on Raasay but he felt it was too small for safety and he sailed back to Skye again. His brief moment of comfort in the MacDonalds' house was like a dream now for he found himself once more hiding in miserable huts and sleeping on the ground.

Captain Malcolm MacLeod had taken over as his guide, and one day the Captain noticed Charles fidgeting. He took him behind a little hill, unfastened his shirt for him and found him 'troubled with lice for want of clean linen'. The Captain was dismayed, but the Prince made light of it as usual, saying that 'the fatigues and distresses he underwent signified nothing at all, because he was a single person; but when he reflected upon the many brave fellows who suffered in his cause, that . . . did strike him to the heart and sink very deep with him'.

Apart from his concern for his supporters, he seemed bewildered about his own future. All his life he had been trained to be a prince and he had been taught to regard himself as the saviour of the British. Even he now had to admit that matters had not turned out as he expected and he was puzzled as to what fate had in store for him. 'I have endured more than would kill a hundred!' he told the Laird of Raasay's sons. 'Surely Providence does not design this for nothing?' On another occasion he turned to his guide, saying, 'MacLeod, do you not think that God Almighty has made this person of mine for doing some good yet?' He could not believe that his mission was to end in failure. These hardships must have a purpose.

'When I was in Italy and dining at the King's table,' he mused, 'very often the sweat would have been coming through my coat with the heat of the climate and now that I am in a cold country, of a more piercing and trying climate, and exposed to different kinds of fatigues, I really find I agree equally with both. I have had this philibeg [kilt] on now for some days and I find I do as well with it as any [of] the best breeches I ever put on. I hope in God, MacLeod, to walk the streets of London with it yet.' Like his mother, he retained a certain childlike simplicity.

He remained a fugitive in Skye for a little longer, until early July, but then he heard that McDonnell of Barrisdale, a powerful MacDonald

150. Map of the Prince's travels, drawn by John Finlayson, an Edinburgh mathematical instrument-maker, who had been in the Jacobite army at Culloden.
(National Museums of Scotland)

chief, had for the time being bought his peace with the government by promising to betray him. This was a dangerous new threat. In great anxiety, he was forced to make his way back to the mainland.

By 10 July Charles was in Borradale once more. That part of the country was swarming with soldiers and it was with the greatest difficulty that his supporters smuggled him past the line of army posts with the notion of taking him further north to Ross-shire. The going was rougher than ever now, and he had to climb high mountains, walk for miles over difficult moorland and sleep in caves or under rocks, every moment in imminent danger of being captured.

On 24 July, he fell in with a group of Jacobite fugitives who were living in a cave in Glenmoriston. The Prince was in tattered highland dress with a hideous yellow wig concealing his own hair, but some of the 'seven men of Glenmoriston' had been in his army and they recognised him at once, falling on their knees before him.

He spent the next six weeks in their company, laughingly referring to them as his 'privy council' and impressing them with his unfailing good humour and his courage. One day a messenger brought word that a French ship had been sighted at Poolewe, forty miles to the north-west. Eagerly he sent out men to investigate, only to discover that the vessel had landed two officers to look for him and then had sailed away again. After this new disappointment, he decided to turn south once more, for he had heard that Lochiel and Macpherson of Cluny were in hiding together in Cameron country.

He travelled by night and hid among the rocks by day, watching the redcoats searching the slopes beneath him. He was often soaked to the skin and after a particularly trying period without food he was so tired and weak that his companions had to support him for the last few miles of the way. Determination drove him on, and finally he reached

153. The cairn at Loch nan Uamh, marking the place where the Prince embarked for France. (Photograph, Dr David Breeze)

Lochiel's house of Achnacarry, only to discover that it had been burned by Cumberland's soldiers. Lochiel was hiding twenty miles further south.

In the end they were reunited on 30 August at a little shieling near Loch Pattack. Lochiel, still limping from his wounds, came out to greet the Prince and would have knelt before him had not Charles prevented him. Someone might see, he said, and his presence would be revealed. They went inside the hut to a feast of fresh mince collops cooked in butter. As he sat eating straight from the saucepan with a silver spoon, Charles gave a sigh of satisfaction. 'Now gentlemen, I live like a Prince!' he declared.

After a few days with Lochiel, Cluny came and took him to his own special hiding place, an ingenious structure of wood, thatch and moss, clinging to the face of a rock. Carefully camouflaged, it would hold six or seven men in comfort and in 'Cluny's Cage' Charles spent the first part of September. Finally, on the 13th, he received the news he had so long awaited. Two French ships had sailed into Loch nan Uamh.

'I hope you are now out of misery', the Prince told his companions, 'but for my part I'd willingly undergo more dangers and hardships than I have done if I could be of any use to you and my poor country!'

Six days later he boarded *Le Prince de Conti* with Lochiel, Dr Archibald Cameron, twenty-one other gentlemen and 107 ordinary men. The Prince later transferred to *L'Heureux*. Cluny Macpherson chose to return to the safety of his cage. That evening the rest set sail for France. Many of them were in tears as they watched Scotland recede into the distance, but they assured each other fervently that they would soon be back, with 'an irresistible force'.

Dipinte in Roma da Domenico Dupra.
Intagliato da N. J. B. De Poilly.
Le Prince Charles Edouard Stuart.
Né à Rome le 31. Decembre 1720.
Edouard presque seul, vole vers ses Etats,   Quel Prince mieux que lui pretend à la Couronne,
Sa fortune et ses droits accompagnent ses pas: Si le sang la transmet, si la vertu la donne.
Se vend à Paris chés N. J. B. De Poilly rue St. Jacques à l'Esperance. 1746.

9

TWO MISTRESSES

TEN DAYS later, the Prince landed at Roscoff in Brittany and went ashore to cheers and a twenty-one gun salute from his ships. His one thought was to travel as quickly as possible to Paris and seek an audience with Louis XV. Not only would he negotiate the military aid he needed; he would ask for the hand in marriage of one of the French princesses. If he were the King's son-in-law no one would dare refuse his demands.

Unfortunately, once he was ashore he found that he was too exhausted to go on. After all the months of privation it was not surprising that he suffered a reaction when he gained safety at last. While he remained at the coast for a few days, a messenger went ahead to announce his arrival and his brother came riding eagerly to meet him. Prince Henry had been living in Paris ever since the cancellation of his expedition and now he took Charles back to his own lodgings.

By this time, the whole city was in a ferment of excitement at his seemingly miraculous reappearance. For months, nothing had been heard of him except vague rumours, and as stories of his endurance and his narrow escapes gradually filtered through, his reputation rose higher and higher. The French people, already discontented with their own government, took up his cause with great enthusiasm, pronouncing that he had been basely betrayed by their ministers.

This valiant Prince had created a diversion in the north, they told each other, thereby making possible their own successes in Flanders, but instead of being grateful, their government had abandoned him. His subsequent defeat at Culloden was their fault, not his. On the streets and in the taverns all the latest gossip was of Charles, not as a defeated general but as a wronged hero, and everyone was eager to see this legendary figure.

At first, the Prince had no interest in the public attitude to his arrival. All his attention was directed towards his audience with Louis and when it seemed a long time in coming he fumed impatiently at the delay. Finally, a message from court arrived, but instead of inviting him to a private meeting, the King graciously summoned both princes to his presence at Versailles on 20 October.* Charles realised the implications right away. If Henry were going as well, no business would be discussed. Worse still, the messenger reminded the Prince that he must make the journey incognito. France was bound by her previous treaty with Britain and she could not be seen to be entertaining any member of the House of Stuart.

---

* New Style

154. Engraving of Charles, with an inscription praising his daring, on sale in Paris in 1746. (National Library of Scotland)

155. Late eighteenth-century engraving of Versailles. (The Mansell Collection Limited)

Charles was exasperated, but he had no choice in the matter. Calling himself 'Baron Renfrew', he set off for Versailles with Henry. He was somewhat mollified by his reception, for Louis broke off a privy council meeting to come and embrace him. At a court where rigid etiquette dictated every move, this was an unmistakable mark of favour.

'My very dear Prince!' the King exclaimed warmly, 'I give thanks to God, who gives me the greatest pleasure of seeing you arrive in good health after so many fatigues and dangers! You have shown that all the

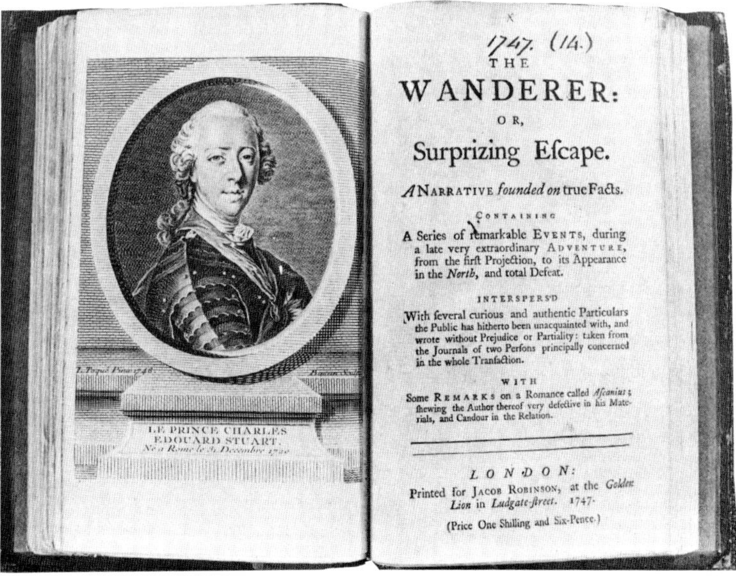

156. Title page of *The Wanderer or Surprizing Escape*, published in 1747, giving an account of the Prince's adventures after Culloden. (National Library of Scotland)

great qualities of heroes and philosophers are united in you!' He then rather spoiled the effect of these gratifying compliments by adding 'and I hope that, one of these days, you will receive the reward of such extraordinary merit'.

This last sentence was the most significant part of his little speech. The Prince was to be rewarded, not now but 'one of these days', and presumably by fate rather than by Louis himself. The French King and his ministers were in fact at that very moment contemplating a peace treaty with George II and nothing was further from their minds than a Jacobite invasion of Britain.

Taken up as he was with the excitement of meeting Louis for the first time, Charles did not realise the full implication of what was being said, and he went away encouraged by the King's friendly manner and confident that the desired private audience would swiftly follow. Ten days later he was bidden to supper with Louis and his family and it seemed to him that, incognito or not, he had been admitted into the charmed royal circle.

He dressed with care for the occasion in a rose pink velvet suit embroidered with silver, the waistcoat of gold brocade. Diamonds sparkled in his white cockade and in his shoe buckles, and the Orders of the Thistle and the Garter gleamed on his breast. According to one admiring observer, 'he glittered all over like the star which they tell you appeared at his nativity'. Further to enhance his own importance he took along with him a group of his commanders: Lord Ogilvy, Lord Elcho, Cameron of Lochiel and several others. Notable by his absence was Lord George Murray. He had made his own way to the continent, travelling to Holland instead of to France and he had no desire for a reunion with the Prince.

157. *Madame de Pompadour*, mistress of Louis XV, by F. Boucher. (National Gallery of Scotland)

158. Fashionable ladies
and gentlemen strolling in
the gardens of the
Tuileries, engraved by
J. Rigaud.
(The Mansell Collection
Limited)

The evening went well. Once more, the King was all affability, the Dauphin could not wait to question Charles about his adventures and the Polish-born Queen, Marie Leszczynska, a distant relative of his own, listened to his description of his sufferings with tears in her eyes. Other such occasions followed and there was even an opportunity to meet Louis in the most informal circumstances. One Sunday, Charles was invited to supper with Madame de Pompadour, the latest royal mistress. During the course of the evening Louis himself arrived, ready to chat to the company in the most relaxed and friendly manner. Yet still no business was mentioned.

By now all the French nobility were alert to the fact that the Prince was in their midst, and 'Baron Renfrew' found himself the centre of attention wherever he went. Invited to balls, concerts, suppers and banquets, he was greeted by the public with delight. When he entered his box at the opera, the audience stood up and applauded. When he strolled in the Tuileries, the crowds cheered. When he arrived at any private funcion, the ladies flocked round him, begging him to tell them yet again about his adventures.

Consoling though it might be, the Prince found all the adulation a tiresome distraction. Fretting over the King's unresponsiveness, he became increasingly irritable and his own father proved to be a further source of annoyance. James III had received the news of his son's deliverance with heartfelt relief but he was now plying him with an endless series of letters giving unwelcome advice. Whatever he did, James warned, he must be careful not to offend the French. Their behaviour in the past might have been far from satisfactory but the time might come when they were willing to contemplate a new invasion of Britain. Until that happened, he must cultivate a philo-sophical attitude as James himself had done, living quietly with Henry Benedict and working hard to gain the favour of the most influential French ministers.

These homilies infuriated the Prince. He was, at the best of times, impatient by nature and now his months of living in concealment had

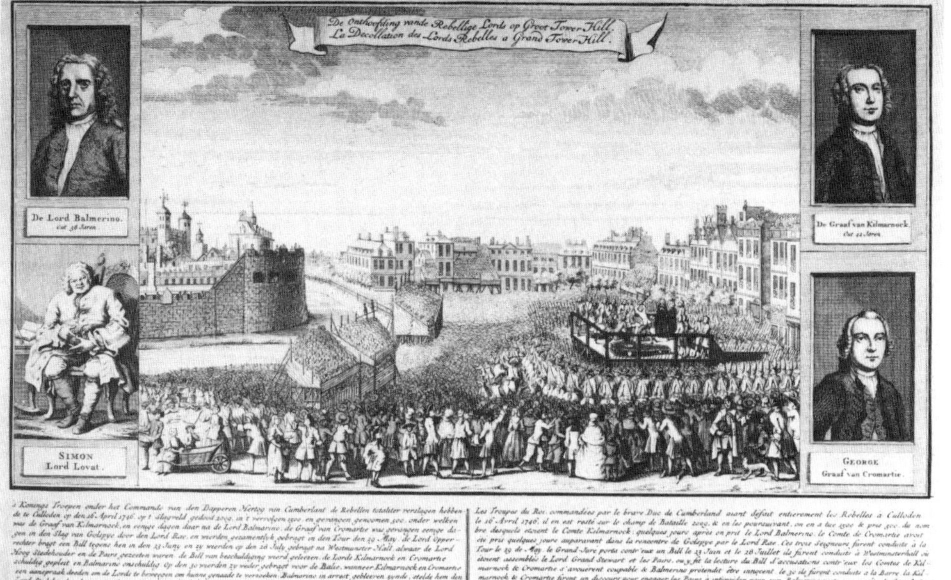

159. Engraving of the execution of the Jacobite earls of Kilmarnock and Cromartie, Lord Balmerino and Lord Lovat, in 1746. (Scottish National Portrait Gallery)

left him in a state of acute nervous tension. To make matters worse, he was daily receiving reports of the execution of his supporters. Desperate to return to Britain in the role of saviour of the nation, he was instead forced to remain becalmed in Paris, all his demands met by bland, smiling evasion. The intrigues of the government sickened him and he took to saying that he was 'only a rough highlander unacquainted with the niceties and refinements of French manners'. In his silks and satins and his powdered wig he could hardly have looked less like one of his clansmen, but the notion of the noble savage was a popular one in French society and no one thought his comments too odd.

That autumn, nothing seemed to be going right. There was the question of his residence, for instance. All his admirers expected Louis XV to install him in a royal palace but instead he was offered a mere financier's house and he refused it angrily. A damaging quarrel was only averted by the intervention of his uncle, the Duke of Bouillon, who found two handsome houses next to his own in the Quai Malaquais, one for Charles and one for Henry.

This arrangement was particularly desirable because the brothers were on increasingly bad terms. During their two-year separation they had grown apart. Charles was no longer the happy, carefree young man of the Muti Palace. Seething with rage and frustration, he all too often vented his ill-humour on Henry, jeering at him for his sober, almost elderly ways and his excessive devotion to religion.

For his part, Henry found that the Prince no longer confided in him. He seemed to prefer the company of Colonel O'Sullivan and the other Irish gentlemen who had rejoined him. He scorned what he saw as Charles's attempts at courting cheap popularity and he was becoming

160. Ring commemorating the executed Jacobite peers.
(National Museums of Scotland)

161. White satin pincushion embroidered with the names of executed Jacobites.
(National Museums of Scotland)

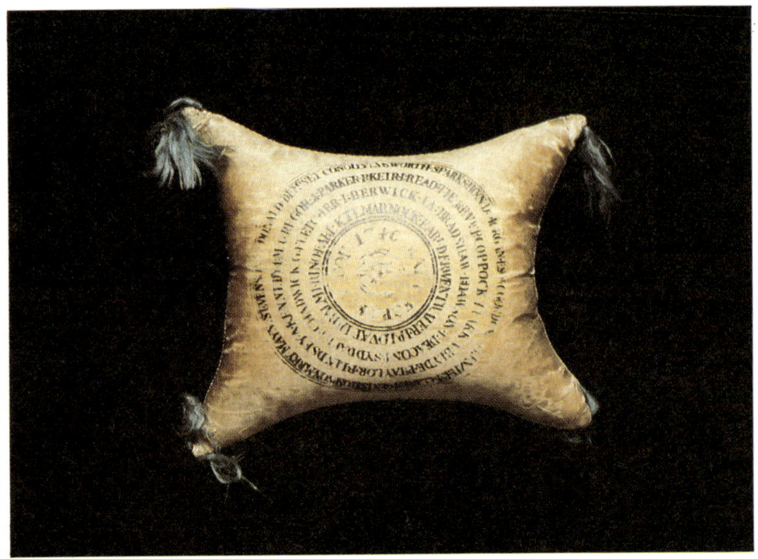

increasingly distressed by the Prince's heavy drinking. The atmosphere between them grew so strained that everyone was relieved when Charles suddenly decided to spend Christmas at Navarre with his uncle's family.

If he seemed more cheerful when he returned, it was not because he was coming to terms with his situation. He had a new plan in mind. He would go to Spain and seek help there. Telling neither Henry nor the French, he travelled secretly to Madrid at the end of January 1747. His sudden appearance threw the Spanish Court into a panic and instead of encouraging him with promises of help or the offer of a royal bride, they urged him to remove his embarrassing presence as quickly as possible.

'I thought there were not such fools as the [French]', Charles told his father, 'but I find it here far beyond it. Your Majesty must forgive me if I speak here a little out of humour, for an angel would take the spleen on this occasion!'

There was nothing for it but to go back to Paris, but instead of returning to his comfortable quarters on the Quai Malaquais, he spent the next month lurking in his banker's house, torturing himself with the thought of all that he could be doing. 'The season is fine,' he wrote wistfully to the French minister of war, 'and the weather is suitable if one wished to undertake something on my behalf. I am always ready and impatient for that happy moment.'

There was no response and the stress began to affect his health. He told people that he found it 'impossible to breathe' in the city, and while this may have been meant metaphorically it could have been a precursor of the asthma which was to plague him in later life. Fortunately, a sympathetic lady lent him her country house at Passy and at the beginning of May he was happily planning the move, his spirits restored.

A week before he was due to go, his brother invited him to dinner and he decided to accept. He arrived at Henry's house to find the candles lit and the servants ready to serve the meal. Of Henry himself, there was no sign. He sat down to wait, and as the minutes ticked by he became increasingly impatient. When one hour passed and then two, his impatience changed to alarm. No one seemed to know where his brother had gone. Eventually he went home, convinced that Henry had been assassinated and it was not until four agonising days later that he received any news. A letter arrived, with his brother's writing on the cover. In a frenzy of anxiety, he tore it open and read the contents with amazed disbelief. He needed a change of air, Henry wrote, and so he was going to Rome to spend a fortnight with their father.

His secretiveness and the abruptness of his departure seemed quite unaccountable to Charles. He himself had left for Madrid in just such a manner, but that was different. As the head of the family in France, he ought to have been informed. The fortnight went by and there was still no sign of Henry but then the Prince received another letter, this time from James III. He would probably not be pleased, his father said, but Henry had taken holy orders. Within a short time, the Pope would make him Cardinal York.

Charles was dumbfounded. Hurling the offending letter from him, he strode into his bedchamber and shut himself in. There he remained, alone, for several hours and when he finally emerged it was to vow that he would never go back to Rome. Never again would he confide in

162. Jacobite wine glasses engraved with the Prince's image and monogram. (National Museums of Scotland)

166. *Henry, Cardinal York,*
painted in Rome in 1748,
by L. G. Blanchet.
(In a Scottish private
collection)

163. Modern bronze copy
of a bust of Charles, by
J. B. Lemoyne, 1746.
(Scottish National Portrait
Gallery)

his family. They had betrayed him, and he was finished with them forever. Henry's name was not to be mentioned in his presence. From that day onwards his letters to his father would be of the briefest: a comment on the weather, an empty expression of obedience but nothing more.

The violence of his reaction was understandable. Henry's decision had wide-ranging political implications and Charles was not the only one to be upset. Jacobites everywhere were furious at this dreadfully damaging blow to their cause. James II had lost the throne of Britain because of his Catholicism and ever since, his son James III had worked hard to convince everyone that he would never attempt to interfere with Britain's established Protestantism should he be restored. His son's open dedication to the Roman Catholic Church made it seem to the world that the Stuarts' sinister intentions remained unaltered

164. Pages from Cardinal
York's Benedictional.
(The Earl of Rosebery)

165. Books belonging to
Cardinal York's famous
library, with his coat of
arms on the binding.
(National Library of
Scotland)

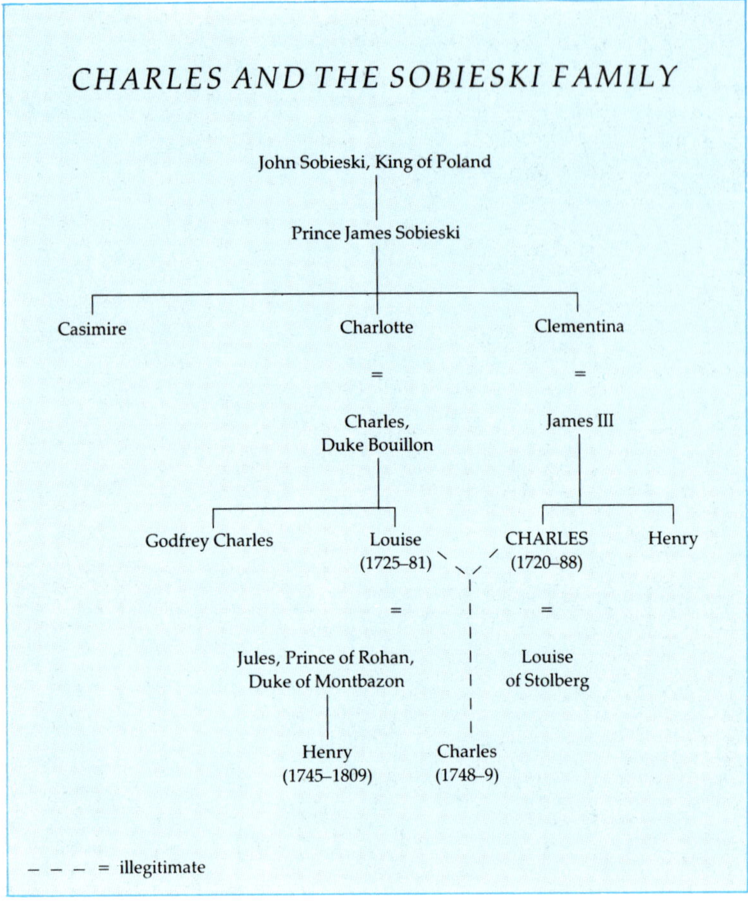

and of course it also meant that the younger Prince could never have an heir. The Hanoverians rejoiced openly at this setback to their enemies' interests.

All his friends were heartily sorry for Charles and they did what they could to divert him. He remained deeply depressed, however, and at the end of August he sought solace in his uncle's house at Navarre. The Duke was still at court and his son was away too, but there was excellent sport to be had, not to mention the sympathetic companionship of his cousin Louise, Duchess of Montbazon.

The Prince had not paid too much attention to Louise before, but now her husband was with the army in Flanders and he found himself spending more and more time in her company. Soon, he was enchanted. She had large, wide-set eyes, a pretty little mouth and an innocent, flirtatious manner. The more he spoke to her, the more Charles realised how much they had in common. Their mothers, both dead now, had been sisters and they shared that ingenuousness which seems to have been a Sobieski characteristic.

Apart from finding themselves naturally in sympathy, they had much to talk about. When she was a child Louise had actually visited

Poland and had spent some time with their grandfather, Prince James Sobieski, and then there were Charles's own reminiscences to discuss. Soon, their mutual attraction became passionate love and as summer ended she became his mistress.

With the coming of autumn, reality impinged on their idyllic life. Louise had to return to Paris, to the house she shared with her mother-in-law in the Place Royale (now the Place des Vosges). Madame de Géméné was a formidable lady in her forties who ruled her establishment with a rod of iron. In the country, it had been easy

167. *Louise, Duchess of Montbazon, Princess of Rohan*, Charles's cousin and mistress, by J. M. Nattier. (The Bibliothèque Nationale, Paris)

168. Detail from a plan showing the Place Royale in 1739. Louise lived in the corner house which is now the Victor Hugo Museum. (The Bibliothèque Nationale, Paris)

enough to elude her, but in town it would be both difficult and dangerous.

Never able to resist a challenge, the Prince told Louise not to worry. His months of concealment in the highlands had given him a taste for disguises, secret plans and the excitement of narrow escapes. He would find a way of continuing their affair. With the help of his valet, he set up an elaborate system of coaches, decoys and incognitos. He travelled in the late evening to Paris, crept up a back stair and joined his cousin in her bedchamber. His stealthy comings and goings aroused the suspicions of the French police, who took him for an assassin plotting the murder of Prince Charles Edward Stuart, but he outwitted them all and continued his nocturnal excursions with even greater relish.

While he plotted and schemed, Louise beguiled her days by writing ardent little notes to him: 'If you were pleased with your night, my love, I confess that for my part I was enchanted . . . Come this evening and live in the arms of her who in the whole world loves only her

169. The Place Royale, engraved in 1752. (The Bibliothèque Nationale, Paris)

dearest love . . .' By December she was pregnant. He was delighted. He would lie beside her, murmuring fond promises of loyalty to both Louise and the coming child. However, there was a new threat to their relationship. Jules, her husband, was due back from the army.

At first, his presence in the Place Royale made little difference. The Prince waited until Jules was in bed before entering the house but it was an uncomfortable business, huddling into his cloak in the cold December night while Jules stayed out late enjoying himself. Moreover, the Prince was soon tortured by jealousy and he began accusing Louise of laughing at him with her husband behind his back. He grew increasingly peevish and, resenting the enforced secrecy, he began to take chances. The result was that Madame de Géméné became suspicious, instructed her servants to keep watch and in the end confronted Louise with her misdoings. In floods of tears, the girl

170. Engraving of L. Toqué's portrait of Charles in 1747, which the Prince gave to Louise. The original picture has vanished but this engraving was done within months of it being painted.
(Scottish National Portrait Gallery)

171. *The Princess of Talmont*, Charles's next mistress, by J. M. Nattier. (Landesmuseum Mainz)

confessed and at her father's dictation she wrote what was supposed to be a farewell letter to the Prince.

'I am required by my duty to them [her family] never to see you again nor even receive your letters', she told him, but she begged him to continue his public visits during the day. If he were suddenly to stop coming everyone would know why, and her reputation would be ruined.

Charles had no intention of complying. He was furious at this latest blow to his self-esteem and instead of calling, as etiquette demanded, he ignored her request. While she wept over his portrait in the privacy of her room, he went out and about to balls as usual, determined to show everyone that he did not care. Louise then took to arriving at events where she knew he would be, but he refused to acknowledge her and turned his head coldly away. Even then she did not give up, but plied him with messages until he agreed to see her one more time.

They met at midnight in a coach in a Paris street, and he told her that there was someone else. She begged him to write to her and he said he would, but he did not, of course, and she finally had to admit that she had lost him. Their child was born on 28 July, a son whom she named Charles. Her husband accepted him as his own, but the baby died six months later.

By that time, the Prince was deeply involved with the lady he had mentioned to Louise. Marie Anne Louise Jablonowska, Princess of Talmont, was forty-seven years old and one of the leading courtesans of the day. Her beauty, her intelligence and her wit had brought her a colourful and exciting career. She was the long-term public mistress of the exiled King Stanislas of Poland and he not only tolerated her other liaisons but obligingly found her a husband. After Louise's tearful

tantrums, her self-possessed sophistication was a pleasant relief and she had all manner of valuable contacts. Within a matter of weeks, Charles became her lover.

It was as well that he had achieved a measure of comfort in his private life, for in the summer a dangerous new crisis threatened his existence in France. International diplomats were in Aix-la-Chapelle trying to bring peace to Europe and one of the provisions of the resulting treaty stipulated that Charles must be ejected from Louis XV's territories.

Everyone had expected that: everyone, except the Prince himself. He refused to accept that he would have to go, for he was convinced that French public opinion would never allow it. The crowds in the parks and at the opera were still his enthusiastic partisans and he went out of his way to charm them into continuing their support.

He also embarked on a series of extravagant gestures designed to show everyone that he was staying. He ordered lavish new furniture for his apartments, told the royal goldsmith to make him an expensive set of plate and then used it at a series of banquets where he assured all the guests that he had no intention of moving.

Louis felt a good deal of sympathy for him, but he could not risk his new-found friendship with George II by allowing him to stay. He did

172. Charles sat for his portrait to M. Q. de la Tour in 1748 and gave the resulting pastel to the Princess of Talmont. This is one of the many versions and copies of it then produced. (Hamilton Collection at Lennoxlove)

173. *James III* by an
unknown artist.
(In a Scottish private
collection)

what he could to soften the blow by apologising to the Prince, offering
him a large pension and suggesting that he could live comfortably in
Switzerland on the proceeds. Charles received this proposal with
disdain. The French King's aged emissary, the Duke of Gesvres, tried
his best on no fewer than three occasions but although his pleas
brought tears to Charles's eyes, the Prince remained immovable.
Finally, the Duke was compelled to issue an ultimatum. If he would
not go willingly, he would be forcibly expelled from France and sent
back to his father in Rome.

That threat affected the Prince as nothing else had done. Turning
pale, he said in a low voice, 'You may be certain that I will not be taken
there alive!' and, leaving the room, he shut himself away in his
chamber, refusing to see anyone.

In a desperate attempt to stave off the inevitable, he let it be known
that he really would kill himself if the King tried to have him arrested.
Believing that this would deter Louis, he then went out and about in
society as usual, impressing all beholders with his gaiety and his
charm. A letter from his father arrived, ordering him to obey the
French King's instructions, but he ignored it. The Princess of Talmont

begged him to submit, but he would not. Finally, on 10 December 1748, Louis signed the order for his banishment. 'Poor Prince!', he sighed, 'How difficult it is for a King to be a true friend!'

The following day, Charles set out for his usual visit to the opera. His coach deposited him in the Rue St Honoré at a narrow lane leading to the opera house. As he stepped forward to stroll down this passage, four men in grey suddenly rushed out, seized him by the arms and carried him bodily through a gateway to the courtyard of the Palais Royal. The entire area was thick with soldiers and his assailants were in fact sergeants in the French army. They searched him and then bound him hand and foot with ten ells of crimson silk cord, specially purchased for the purpose. White-faced, he protested, but they told him that it was for his own good, to prevent him from harming himself.

He was bundled unceremoniously into a hired coach and taken to the state prison of Vincennes. They placed him in a small cell while his house was searched and the principal members of his retinue were consigned to the Bastille. He would be allowed to go free, he was told, if he agreed to leave the country. Otherwise, he would be taken as a prisoner to Rome and handed over to James III.

As far as he was concerned, there was no choice. He promised to go and early on the morning of 15 December he was released. A military escort accompanied him as far as Fontainebleau, where he announced that he was too ill to travel. He had certainly been suffering from nausea and coughing fits, but he was probably playing for time. He tried to see the Princess of Talmont, but that was not possible, and on 23 December he finally left France.

174. Coin box belonging to James III. Its contents include a large medal of Charles, as well as coins struck when James touched sufferers from scrofula, or the King's Evil. (In a private collection)

10
LOCHABER NO MORE

THE PRINCE now embarked upon a lengthy period of concealment, long years of wandering through France, Switzerland, Germany and the Low Countries under a series of assumed names and usually in disguise. He became variously John Douglas, the Chevalier Thompson, Mr William Smith, Mr Mildmay, Mr Burton and Mr Benn. Sometimes he was a priest with a black eyepatch, sometimes an English doctor travelling for the sake of his health. Sometimes he grew his beard and sometimes he wore a long false nose. He was such a master of disguise that even people who knew him well failed to recognise him and all the while he kept up a constant correspondence with would-be friends and supporters, writing to them in an assumed hand, or with what he hoped was invisible ink.

Of course, these precautions were in many ways necessary. The British government was desperate to keep track of his movements and there was a very real danger that secret agents might assassinate him. Apart from that, however, he seems to have become obsessed with the excitement of life as a fugitive and he simply could not settle down to the normal daily round.

If the French thought that they had seen the last of him, they were mistaken. He had no intention of living meekly in Switzerland or anywhere else. Life in exile was not for him: this was merely another strategic withdrawal. He went first to Avignon, papal territory and therefore not out of bounds to him. There he lodged with Lady Inverness until the Archbishop provided him with a suitable residence. Welcomed by local society, he attended supper parties and masked balls. If he had confined himself to conventional entertainments, all might have been well, but he insisted on introducing boxing matches to the city. A previous Pope had outlawed this particular sport from Avignon and so he was soon embroiled in a heated quarrel with both the Archbishop and the Pope. When the British government began to utter threats against the papal authorities for harbouring him, the Archbishop asked him to leave.

The Princess of Talmont had been anxiously watching his progress from Paris and now she came to the rescue. She had a house in Lorraine, where her old lover King Stanislas kept his court, and in no time at all Charles was in the area, lodging with the King's physician. For the next three years, he divided his time between Lorraine and Paris. In the Rue St Dominique in the capital stood the Convent of St Joseph. As well as accommodation for the nuns, it had comfortable apartments which were rented to aristocratic ladies. The old Marquise de Deffand, patron of Voltaire and Montesquieu, lived there, as did the Princess's friend Elisabeth Ferrand, a young lady of intellectual tastes.

175. Avignon, the Papal Square with the Papal Palace and Notre Dame de Dom Cathedral.
(James Davis Library)

Now the Princess herself took a suite of rooms and for weeks on end she and her sympathetic friends concealed the Prince in a small upstairs chamber. When he was away in Lorraine, they sent him books, supplied him with news and acted as his intermediaries with the King. Louis knew all about his presence in France, but it suited him to turn a blind eye to it. The day might yet come when he could prove useful.

Charles himself spent much of his time planning a return to Britain and in the summer of 1750 he went so far as to order his agent in Antwerp to purchase 26,000 muskets and 10,000 swords. At the same time, he asked his father to renew his commission as Regent. Telling him sadly that he was 'a continual heartbreak', James complied. That September, the Prince set out secretly to reconnoitre the situation for himself. He arrived in London on 16 September and spent the next week in the city, touring the outside of the Tower of London to inspect its defences. He even appeared at a party being given by Lady Primrose, a Scottish Jacobite, much to her alarm. He then went to 'the new church in the Strand', announced that he had abandoned Roman Catholicism and joined the Church of England.

Even this startling move did not win him any more support, and by the end of the month he was back in Paris again, morose, ill-tempered and quarrelsome. He had argued before with the Princess, but now their disagreements became so frequent and so noisy that the other residents in the convent began to complain. Finally, after one particularly spectacular difference of opinion, the Princess declared that she never wanted to see him again, and he was asked to go. Declaring huffily that it would be cheaper for him to live in the Netherlands, he set off for Ghent.

Even after the fiasco of his London trip, he cherished hopes of a return to Britain and late that autumn he visited Berlin where he tried to enlist the help of Frederick the Great. Frederick received him with no more than politeness but he left again convinced that Prussia meant to help him. He had been writing to Scandinavia, too, and the Swedish apparently promised to assist. A new plot was conceived in conjunction with Lord Elibank's brother, Alexander Murray. This involved a two-pronged attack on Britain, with a body of Swedish troops arriving in Scotland while the English Jacobites rose and deposed George II. The Prince was so optimistic that he told people that 'he expected to be in London very soon himself, and that he was determined to give the present government no quiet until he succeeded or died in the attempt'.

He did not realise, of course, that among the conspirators was a Hanoverian spy, known to the British government as 'Pickle'. In reality, this was Alastair MacDonnell, Young Glengarry. On the surface, Glengarry appeared to be all enthusiasm for the Elibank Plot but he was privately relaying every last detail to George II. In the end, the English Jacobites got wind of the fact that their secret was known, and they hastily abandoned all thought of a rising.

Charles was plunged into despair once more, and there was little consolation to be found in his private life. Still refusing to accept a pension from the French, he had been reduced to paying off his servants and selling some of his personal belongings. At this low point in his life, he suddenly received a letter from an old friend. Clementina Walkinshaw was in the Netherlands and she was anxious to see him.

The motives for her unexpected reappearance have never been satisfactorily explained. She herself claimed that when Charles left her at Bannockburn House he made her promise to come to him if he ever needed her. Whether he did summon her is unknown. She had come ostensibly to take up a position in a convent in the Netherlands and it may be that on her arrival his friends urged her to get in touch with him again. Perhaps she could rouse him from his melancholy. At any rate, he wrote back to her, arranged to meet her secretly in Paris and seemed overjoyed at their reunion. In no time at all she was his mistress, and they travelled back to Ghent together to live as man and wife.

Under other circumstances, Clementina might have provided Charles with the steadying influence he so badly needed, but there were too many difficulties from the start. Not only did they have to keep moving about, under a variety of aliases, but the Jacobites soon became jealous of her intimacy with the Prince and it was not long before they remembered her unsuitable Hanoverian connections. Her sister the lady-in-waiting was obviously a supporter of the British government. Clementina, they were quick to point out, was probably a spy.

That was bad enough, but life with Charles proved increasingly upsetting. He was thirty-four now. Nearly ten years had passed since his departure for Scotland, and his situation was going from bad to worse. The once elegant Prince who had dazzled at balls and operas was reduced to maintaining a wardrobe consisting of only three suits. His English supporters were heartily tired of his endless demands for money and they were becoming increasingly alienated by his erratic behaviour and his bad temper. 'They expect a Prince who will take advice and rule according to law, and not one that thinks his will sufficient,' his equerry warned him, but to no avail.

When he was not haunting the taverns in search of visitors with news from England, he was sitting moodily at home, sunk in gloom. 'I am a sedentary man', he told one acquaintance drearily, 'The gazettes is an amusement to me.' Even the birth of his daughter on 27 October 1753 brought only temporary rejoicing. He carried her to the church himself and had her christened Charlotte, but a month later he was quarrelling bitterly with Clementina about religion, wrestling with his financial difficulties and crying desperately 'I suffocate!'

Even the Bouillon family became concerned about him. His uncle, the Duke, had been deeply hurt by the affair with Louise but he was dead now and his son offered Charles the use of a pretty little castle at Bouillon. He moved Clementina and their child there and for a time he

176. An ecclesiastical history belonging to Charles, with his special binding. It is Stefano Evodio Assemani's *De Pontifice Maximo post obitum Clementis XIII*. (National Library of Scotland)

seemed his old self again, shooting and fishing happily on the estate. Unfortunately, this rural peace was shattered by a message from Paris. The French were at war with Britain once more and they had a suggestion which might interest him.

Excitedly, he set off for the capital and found lodgings above a butcher's shop. He ventured out only at night, and for some days he heard nothing. Eventually, however, he was invited to a secret rendezvous and a government envoy divulged what was in the ministers' minds. They were planning a new invasion of England, it seemed, and they would be pleased if Charles created a diversion in either Scotland or Ireland.

The Prince had been deceived too often before to be trapped into that unrewarding situation. He suspected that the French were not really interested in winning back Britain for the Stuarts. They merely wanted to keep George II's realm in a state of perpetual conflict by setting Charles up as, say, Regent of Scotland. It was not enough. They must make him Regent of Britain. 'No division!' he replied. 'All or nothing!'

There ensued a lengthy silence. Confident that they could do nothing without him, he waited. When summer came, he travelled to Brest to watch the French fleet assembling. It all had a horrible air of familiarity about it, and when the ministers proposed that he should set sail for Scotland with perhaps two or three ships instead of going with the main expedition, he refused angrily. It was late October before the French finally moved. In wild waters in Quiberon Bay, the

British fleet intercepted Admiral Conflans and defeated him soundly. The last serious attempt at an invasion was over.

Back to Bouillon went the Prince, furious, hurt and ready to strike out at anyone who came near him. Drink was his only consolation. Indeed, he had long shown all the classic symptoms of alcoholism: the early ability to drink everyone else under the table while he remained apparently unaffected, the later consumption of vast quantities of wine, brandy, beer and sherry and at last a failure to eat, self-neglect, unreasoning suspicion and violent outbursts of rage. He and his brother had fierce tempers, even in childhood. Henry learned to control his: Charles relied on his charm to earn him pardon.

Now all the charm had gone. He was, one of his supporters complained, 'unforgiving, and revengeful for the very smallest offence', quite often drinking so much that he seemed 'in some degree devoid of reason'. The considerate Prince who had treated Flora MacDonald with such care had become a bullying domestic tyrant. He adored his little daughter, whom he called 'Pouponne', but to Clementina he was hostile and abusive. She was, she told him sadly, 'the victim in everything that disobliged you'. Eventually, she could stand it no longer and in July 1760 she left him, taking six-year-old Charlotte with her to a convent in Paris.

Her parting letter explained. 'Your Royal Highness cannot be surprised', she wrote, '. . . when you consider the repeated bad treatment I have met with these eight years past, and the daily risk of losing my life. Not being able to bear any longer such hardships, my health being altered by them has obliged me at last to take this desperate step . . . There is not a woman in the world that would have suffered so long as what I have done.' In spite of everything, she still loved him, or at least the man he had once been and, she said, 'I quit my dearest Prince with the greatest regret and shall always be miserable if I don't hear of his welfare and happiness'.

Determined to cut her out of his life, Charles uttered not one word of dismay at her departure, but he did lament the loss of his daughter Pouponne. 'I shall be in the greatest affliction until I get back the child, which was my only comfort in my misfortune', he told one of his few remaining friends, and he sent men to try to snatch her back. They failed, Louis XV accorded Clementina and Charlotte his protection and James III agreed to pay them a pension in spite of the fact that he had always disapproved of the relationship. Charles thereupon decided that his father was to blame for Clementina's defection and he did not hesitate to tell everyone so.

James, in fact, had nothing to do with the whole sorry business. He tried to calm Charles by pointing out that Pouponne would be better-educated in her convent than under 'the uncertain and ambulatory life you lead'. He had long since given up trying to understand, let alone control, his son's erratic behaviour and his piteous pleas that Charles should at least pay him a visit were consistently ignored.

Alone at Bouillon, the Prince drank heavily, refused to eat and would not go out. Clementina herself was alarmed at the rumours she

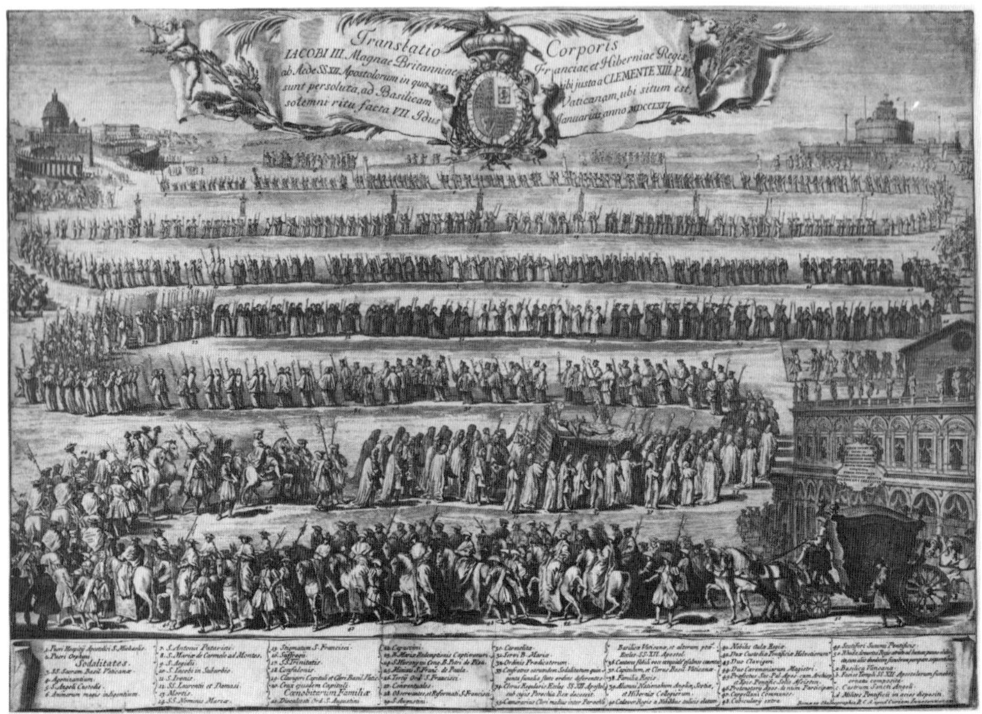

177. Engraving of the funeral procession of James III, 1766. (Scottish National Portrait Gallery)

heard about him. Just after Christmas she wrote to him in concerned tones assuring him that 'nothing in this world can be more sensible to me than this fatal separation', and she added, 'I can't express to you, my Dearest Prince, how much my heart suffers on this account'.

By the following February, she was even more worried. She had heard reports that 'You are not yourself, that your head is quite gone'. The one stable relationship in his life over, Charles had reached the depths of despair. As Lord Elibank told him, 'Your Royal Highness is resolved to destroy yourself to all intents and purposes. Everybody here talks of your conduct with horror, and from being once the admiration of Europe you have become the reverse.'

Slowly, the years went by. In 1760, George II died and was succeeded peacefully by his grandson George III. Two years later, James III suffered a stroke which left him unable to do any more business. Still the Prince refused to go and see him. The old King lived on for a further three and a half years but by Christmas 1765 it was obvious that the end was near. Henry Benedict, Cardinal York, sent urgent messages to Bouillon and at last Charles decided to go south. He was too late to see his father alive. James died peacefully on 1 January 1766 and thereafter the Prince was known to the Jacobites as Charles III.

His father's little court had awaited his arrival with mixed feelings. They had heard such highly-coloured accounts of his dissipation that when they finally saw him they were pleasantly surprised. It was true

178. *Andrew Lumisden*, the Prince's secretary: a paste medallion made in 1784 by James Tassie.
(Scottish National Portrait Gallery)

179. Snuffbox given to Andrew Lumisden by Cardinal York, when Charles dismissed him. (National Museums of Scotland)

that he looked far older than his forty-six years, with his stout body, his swollen legs and his red, puffy face, but in spite of his lethargic manner they thought that they could see in him traces of what he had once been. One observer commented, 'When a young man, he must have been extremely handsome', and his father's secretary, Andrew Lumisden, remarked, 'He charms everyone who approaches him'.

After an absence of more than twenty years, Charles established himself in the Muti Palace, went out shooting, listened to music and took to playing the French horn. 'I am persuaded', said his brother, 'we should gain ground as to everything, were it not for the nasty bottle that goes on but too much and certainly must at last kill him.'

The initial excitement of his return over, he found himself leading a solitary life. The Pope was refusing to recognise his royal status and he was forced to style himself Count of Albany. No one really knew how to address him and so Roman society stayed away. He was pathetically glad to see those visitors who did call, and when Sir William Hamilton, the British envoy at Naples, went to the Muti Palace in the spring of 1767, he found him 'absorbed in melancholy thoughts, a good deal of distraction in his conversation and frequent brown studies . . . He told me time lay heavy upon him. I said I supposed he read a good deal. He made no answer'.

As time passed, he grew restless. He fretted about the Pope's unco-operativeness and toyed with the idea of moving to Florence. Even at this late stage he was still ready for one final cloak and dagger excursion to relieve the monotony of his existence. In 1771, Louis XV

180. Letter written by Cardinal York in 1767, commenting that if Charles 'could but get the better of the nasty bottle, which every now and then comes on by spurts, I would hope a great deal of our gaining a good deal as to other things . . .' (National Library of Scotland)

181. *The Sins of the Drunkard*, a pamphlet written by Cardinal York. This is a modern edition; no eighteenth-century copy has been traced. (National Library of Scotland)

Frascati. may. ye 20th 1767.

These few lines will only serve to accuse the receipt of your's of the 7th. have no time to write at length. My B: was to dine with me last thursday, I found him very well pleased of his visit to the Pope and particularly to of his haveing had in that occasion a present from his Holiness of a pair of Beads of such a kind as are only given to Sovrains, and cou'd not but get the better of the nasty Bottle which every now and then comes on by spurts, I wou'd hope a great deal of our gaining a good deal as to other things but I see that to get the better of that nasty Habit there must be the hand of God. I have nothing else remarquable to mention to you, so make an end with the usual assurances &c.

4

he deliberately coöperates in the grievous sin of another.

10. Whosoever is guilty of excess and intemperance in drinking, even though not to intoxication, but thereby causing great distress to his family, squandering away by his intemperance that which should serve for their support, commits a mortal sin against charity and justice. In like manner, whosoever thus renders himself incapable of the payment of his debts, although he may not drink to intoxication, commits a mortal sin.

Let all confessors, both secular and regular, impress upon their penitents the enormity of this sin, by some, perhaps, little regarded, and let them diligently prescribe the means for its correction. As to habitual and relapsing sinners, let those rules be observed which a prudent confessor should follow with such a class of penitents, by deferring absolution till he sees effectual improvement in the correction of the evil habits.

Catholic Truth Society, 18 West Square, London, S.E.

Price 1s. per 100.

3

THE CARDINAL DUKE OF YORK ON

The Sins of the Drunkard.

[HENRY, Cardinal Duke of York, was the second son of James Stuart, known as "the Pretender," and was born at Rome, March 26th, 1725. He spent almost all his life in the Eternal City, and was made Cardinal in 1747 by Pope Benedict XIV. He was a studious and well-informed prince, and a sincerely pious prelate. The following paper from his pen is ordered to be read in every church and chapel in the Diocese of Liverpool on the first Sunday of February and July, and is well worth attentive perusal.]

IN consequence of the widely-spread vice of Intemperance, and the many evils, both spiritual and temporal, resulting from it, we feel it incumbent

---

2

upon us to make known to all the following doctrines, the teaching of our gravest theologians:

1. Whosoever deliberately drinks to such an extent as to lose his reason commits a mortal sin.

2. Whosoever knows by past experience that a certain quantity of liquor has rendered him intoxicated, if he again drinks to the same degree, whereby he does, can, and ought to foresee that drunkenness will ensue, commits a mortal sin.

3. Whosoever continues to drink, notwithstanding his probable belief that intoxication will be the result, and notwithstanding that he foresees or ought to foresee this danger, commits a mortal sin.

4. Whosoever knows by past experience that when drunk he is accustomed to blaspheme, or utter other improper language, or to strike other individuals about him—besides the mortal sin of drunkenness, is guilty of those other crimes, either mortal or venial, committed during the state of intoxication.

5. Whosoever knows by past experience that by frequenting alehouses, gin-shops, and taverns, or

---

3

by going thither in company with others, he is generally accustomed to fall into drunkenness, is obliged under mortal sin to avoid the proximate occasion of sin—that is, to abstain from frequenting such alehouses, gin-shops, or taverns, or from going thither with such companions.

6. Whosoever goes to confession, and has not a true and firm resolution of so abstaining in the cases aforesaid, cannot be absolved; and should he receive absolution, it is not only of no avail, but he becomes guilty of sacrilegious confession.

7. Whosoever does not adopt the proper means for the correction of this vicious habit of drunkenness commits another mortal sin, distinct from the actual sin of drunkenness, and moreover remains in a continual state of sin.

8. Whosoever entices and urges another to excess in drinking, whom he foresees will be intoxicated, commits a mortal sin.

9. Any seller of liquor, who continues to supply it to an individual who he knows will become intoxicated therewith, commits a mortal sin, because

thought of a new way of annoying the British and he invited Charles to Paris once more.

Off he went, disguised as 'the Chevalier Douglas', to lodge secretly in a tailor's house until this latest venture was explained to him. It seemed a pity that the Stuart line should be allowed to end with him, said the French. Why did he not marry? After all, he was still only fifty. He hardly cut a romantic figure, but there must be plenty of young women willing to overlook his deficiencies for the sake of becoming Queen of Great Britain.

The offer of a lavish pension dispelled any lingering doubts Charles might have had and he decided to send Colonel Edmund Ryan, an Irish Jacobite, to the courts of Germany to find him a suitable wife. The first young lady the Colonel interviewed burst into hysterical tears when he explained his mission but that winter he came upon another candidate who had no such scruples.

182. *Charles* in 1770, aged forty-nine, by L. Pecheux. This picture later belonged to Cardinal York. (Stanford Hall, Lutterworth, near Rugby: photograph, Courtauld Institute of Art)

183. *Henry, Cardinal York
at morning prayer in Rome,*
1773, by the Scottish artist
David Allan.
(Department of Prints and
Drawings, National
Gallery of Scotland)

Louise of Stolberg was almost twenty, an unusual beauty with
dazzling white skin, fair hair and dark eyes. She had 'a good figure,'
Ryan told Charles, 'a pretty face and excellent teeth, with all the
qualities which Your Majesty can desire'. She was also willing, indeed,
eager to become his bride. Her father had died young, leaving her
impoverished mother with four young daughters to raise. After a
convent education, Louise had been launched upon society with the
sole aim of finding a wealthy husband. Now it seemed that this
ambition was about to be fulfilled beyond even her expectations.

The marriage contract was rapidly drawn up and signed. Not only
did it settle Louise's future financial position, but it stipulated that the
union was to be consummated on the very day that she and Charles
met. This desirable bridegroom was not going to be allowed any time
for second thoughts. Their proxy marriage was celebrated in Paris at
the end of March 1772 and then Colonel Ryan escorted Louise to
Macerata, where Charles was waiting. On 17 April they met and
married in the Marefoschi Palace. Louise was a Catholic and Charles
had long since cast aside his brief allegiance to the Church of England.
Cardinal Marefoschi therefore performed the ceremony. Five days
later, Charles and Louise arrived in Rome.

Everyone was eager to see the new bride, and a stream of all the
city's most fashionable inhabitants hurried to the Muti Palace. They
were all greatly taken with Louise, who soon earned the affectionate
title, 'The Queen of Hearts'. Charles made an effort, stayed sober and
escorted her to concerts and operas. Cardinal York was approving,
and won the gratitude of the bride by pressing into her hand a gold
snuffbox set with diamonds. Inside it was a bank draft for 40,000
crowns.

184. *Louise of Stolberg*, wife of Charles. This is a miniature by an unknown artist, set in the St Andrew Order of the Thistle. It later belonged to Cardinal York and is now kept with the Scottish Regalia in Edinburgh Castle.
(By gracious permission of Her Majesty The Queen)

One person who was not pleased was Clementina Walkinshaw. Apart from anything else, the death of James III had meant the end of her pension and now she came to Rome in person with her daughter to demand financial assistance. Charles refused to see her. He did indicate that he was willing to take Pouponne into his household, provided that she sever all links with her mother, but she refused to do that. Cardinal York rescued them from this impasse by offering to provide them with an income. At that, they departed back to Paris.

Possibly this episode stirred up all Charles's former resentments. At any rate, it was not long before he was drinking again, and Louise made little attempt to conceal her cold distaste for him. In 1774, he decided to move to Florence, and there they settled down to a gloomy, depressing existence. He walked by the Arno alone, drove his wife round the city, took her to the theatre and fell asleep during the performances. His once splendid health was in ruins. He was deaf, he had asthma, dropsy and continual sickness. Louise, wretchedly trapped in his trying company, longed for him to die and set her free.

In 1777, he bought the San Clemente Palace in the Via San Sebastiano and on its roof he defiantly erected a weathervane bearing the date and the initials CR: Carolus Rex. His wife found some consolation in gathering around her a little circle of poets and artists. They sat and talked about literature while Charles dozed in the background. To these salons came Count Vittorio Alfieri, a romantic young poet of twenty-seven. He and Louise fell in love, and when Charles dropped off to sleep they crept away to her bedchamber together. Eventually, Charles realised what was happening and on

185. *A Panoramic View of Florence in 1775*, by Thomas Patch. (Yale Center for British Art: Paul Mellon Collection)

186(*a*) The San Clemente Palace in Florence, where Charles and his wife lived: entrance.
(*b*) facade.
(Fotostudio Cosci)

187 Painted ceiling in the palace, with the arms of 'Charles III'.
(*b*) detail.
(Fotostudio Cosci)

188. *Charles*, 'drawn from nature at Florence, 1778' by Ozias Humphrey. (A. Stirling of Keir)

St Andrews Night 1780, after an evening of heavy drinking, he forced his way into her room, accused her of adultery and attacked her. Hearing her screams, the servants hurried to the rescue.

Next morning, Louise decided that she could stand it no longer and she and Alfieri plotted her escape. One day not long afterwards, she told Charles that she and a lady friend were going to see some lace being made in a nearby convent. Predictably, Charles insisted on going along too, but when they got there she whisked inside and he was left on the steps as the door slammed in his face. All his shouts and protests were in vain. A few days later she set off for Rome.

There, she had no difficulty in enlisting the sympathetic support of both Cardinal York and the Pope. All she wanted to do, she said, was to live peacefully in a convent. Cardinal York knew only too well how

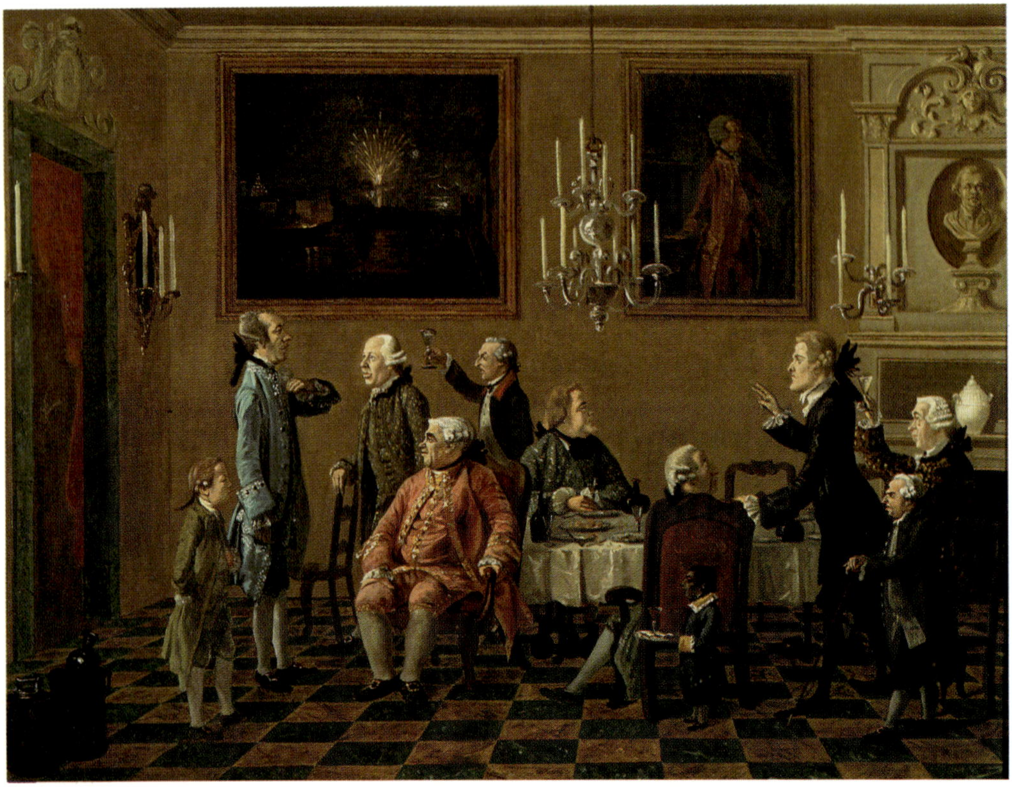

189. *A Dinner Party at Sir Horace Mann's in Florence*, about 1763–5. Sir Horace, the tall man on the left, sent back to the British government regular reports about Charles's behaviour during his years in Florence.
(Yale Center for British Art: Paul Mellon Collection)

Florence ye 18 July 1777 — Mr Innes,
I received in due time yrs of ye 9 June, and do not in ye Least doubt of yr following ye fut-steps of yr Ancestors, ho were Subjects I knue already; the Late King my Father had a par-ticular reguard for. It gives me a real pleasure to here how your new Principal is so well qualified to remplace the moste worthy decesed Mr Gordon whose death gave me Concern, as it was a great Loss to owr Scotch Colege at Paris; my good wishes be-ing always for their welfere, assuring both you and them, of my Protection; I do remain yr Sincere Friend, Charles R.
For Mr Henry Innes Procurator of ye Scotch College of Paris.

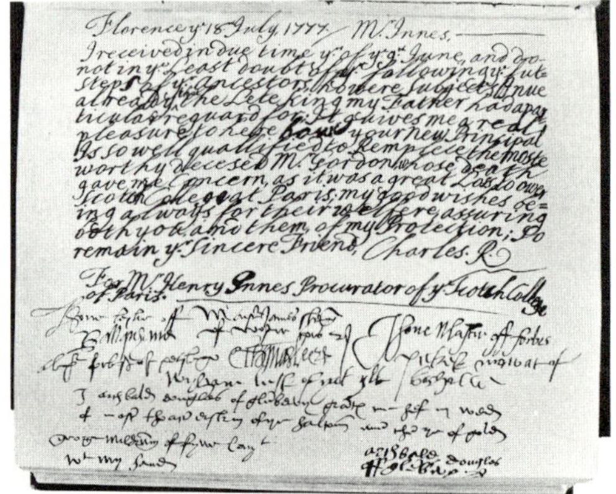

190. Letter written by Charles in 1777, at the age of fifty-six, congratulating the new principal of the Scots College in Paris on his appointment.
(From a facsimile in the Scottish Catholic Archives)

difficult his brother could be and he arranged that she should have half the money usually paid to Charles. He was glad, too, when she began to go out and about a little in society, and he enjoyed entertaining her to dinner. Sometimes she brought along her pleasant, intellectual friend Count Alfieri, and they had stimulating conversations about books and poetry. Not for one moment did he suspect that she and the Count were lovers.

The deception lasted for nearly two years. Finally, in 1783, Charles fell so seriously ill that he was given the Last Rites and Henry came

191. Louise and Alfieri, painted by their friend F. X. Fabre after they had settled down together. (From a reproduction in the Scottish National Portrait Gallery Archive)

192. Monument by A. Canova to Count Alfieri, in the Church of S. Croce, Florence, 1810. The inscription makes reference to Louise. (Photograph, Scala)

193. Monument to Louise of Stolberg in the Church of S. Croce, Florence, 1824. (Photograph, Alinari)

hurrying to Florence to see him. Contrary to all expectation, his brother recovered and while he was convalescing he told Cardinal York about Louise and the Count. Furious at having been deceived, Henry told the Pope, who immediately arranged to have Alfieri banished from Rome.

Louise retired huffily to the country, pined for her lover and reviled her husband to anyone willing to listen. Finally, their marriage ended in an unexpected way. King Gustavus III of Sweden, travelling through Italy, came upon Charles and was touched by his miserable

condition. He decided that he must do something to help and he persuaded Louise to agree to a legal separation. If she gave up all her financial claims on Charles, she would be at liberty to go and live where she pleased. She would not be free to marry again, for this was a separation, not a divorce, but the French offered to pay her a pension. Delighted with the arrangement, she set off to meet Alfieri. They lived together until his death in 1803, whereupon she moved in with the French artist Fabre. She died in 1824.

Charles in the meantime was vastly relieved, for his financial position had improved enormously. He also had a new interest in life. While he was recovering from his grave illness of 1783, his thoughts turned to his daughter. He would have no other children now. There would be no sons to carry on the Stuart line. Why should he not make her his successor instead of Henry, whose whole life was devoted to the church? As soon as he was well enough, he instructed his lawyers to draw up a document making Charlotte legitimate, and in the summer of 1784, after another serious illness, he sent for her. She was to come and live with him.

Little Pouponne was thirty years old now, and a woman of some experience. After her careful convent education she had embarked

CHARLES AND HIS DESCENDANTS

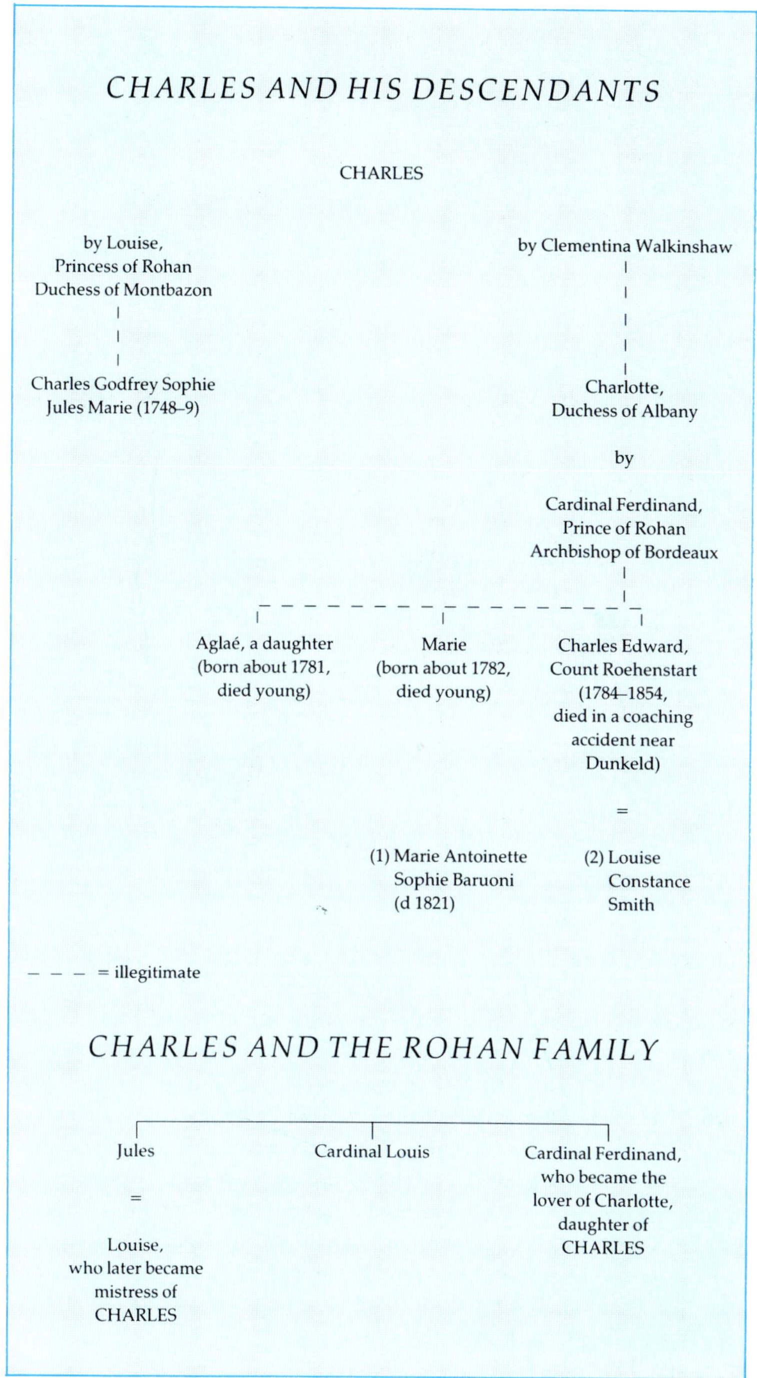

CHARLES AND THE ROHAN FAMILY

upon a longstanding affair with a French cardinal of the Rohan family.
She had already borne him two daughters, Aglaé and Marie, and
when her father's invitation arrived she had just given birth to a son.
She named him Charles Edward.

195. *Charlotte, Duchess of Albany*, Charles's daughter, painted in 1785 by Hugh Douglas Hamilton. (Scottish National Portrait Gallery)

Contemplating the unexpected message from Italy, she hardly knew what to do. The thought of leaving her children, not to mention the Cardinal, filled her with dismay and yet it was what she had always wanted. Not surprisingly, she and her mother shared a strong emotional bond and it had long been their ambition to make Charles recognise his responsibilities towards them. Clementina Walkinshaw was still eking out her meagre pension in a convent and Charlotte's own offspring faced an uncertain future because of their unconventional parentage. If she went to Florence, she could persuade her father to make financial provision for them all. Surely that was worth a brief absence from Paris? Everyone said that Charles had only a few months more to live. In no time at all, she could be back again, settling down to a secure future. She decided to go.

Sending her infant son to a wet-nurse in the country and leaving the two little girls with her mother, she set off for Florence that autumn. A tender reunion ensued. Her father was delighted with her. He made her Duchess of Albany and on St Andrews Night he presented her with the Order of the Thistle. He was hardly fit for an active social life, but he took her out to the opera, gave small parties and loved to show

Gask Septr 29
1755

My Dear Aunt

Papa had a letter from Mr Henry Nairne dated Florence Agust 12th he says "I have the pleasure to acquaint you that ———: ——— keeps our far beyond expectation, if he continues on the same diet that he keeps at present, & I have great reason to imagine he will, he may live many years — he does not forget his good old friends & acquaintances he desires to be properly remembered to them, his Daughter is realy an amiable young woman she is profsest of most noble & generous sentiments I have had many proofs of her feeling & sensibility for the poor & afflicted, she is esteemed & admired by every person here that knows her — tho' the diminution of my friends & relations be great yet I am persuaded they are too numerous to be all named in a Letter — I shall therefore only mention

her off. Even this modest activity was too much for him, however, and in January he collapsed with what his doctors diagnosed as a fatal inflammation of the brain. Charlotte nursed him carefully and once more he surprised them all by recovering. When spring came, he was happily making plans to take his daughter to Rome, while she sorted out his chaotic finances, ordered expensive new clothes and wrote twice-weekly letters to her mother, begging for news of the Cardinal and their children.

That autumn Charles and she travelled south and settled down in the Muti Palace. If people had been eager to see his wife, they were even more curious about his daughter, 'a French lady, who for thirty years had been totally neglected but who, on a sudden, was transformed into a Duchess', as one bystander put it. Charlotte was scrutinised with all the more fascination because she was clad in the latest Parisian fashions and it was decided that she was 'of a good figure, tall and well-made'. She could not be called handsome, because 'the features of her face resemble too much those of her father', but in spite of that disadvantage she was 'gay, lively, very affable and has the behaviour of a well-bred Frenchwoman'.

196. Letter to Lady Robertson of Lude from her nephew in Rome, reporting that Charlotte is 'really an amiable young woman'.
(Scottish Record Office)

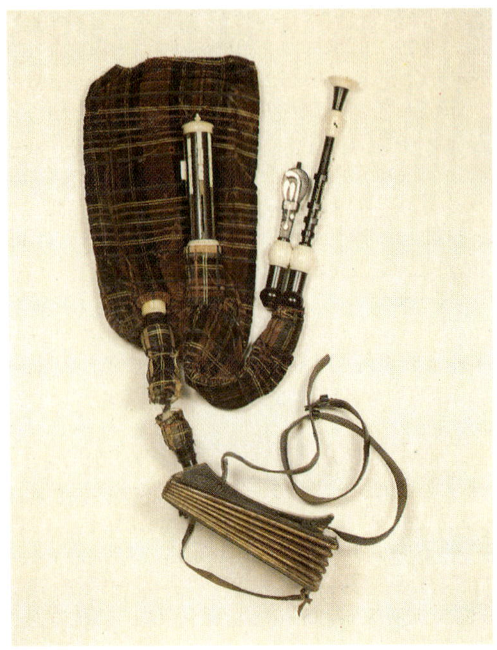

197. Set of French bagpipes which probably belonged to Charles: they were later sold with Cardinal York's belongings. They were not blown with the lips but inflated by the small bellows, held under the arm.
(National Museums of Scotland)

Even so, Charlotte's life was hardly carefree. Putting her father's finances in order took far longer than she had hoped and she had to work hard to gain the confidence of Cardinal York. Her uncle at first suspected her of being a fortune-hunter, but as he came to know her, his liking for her grew. He did refuse when Charles asked him to adopt her. That was going too far. However, he was friendly enough otherwise and he and Charlotte became anxious allies, conspiring together to do what they could to make life happier for her father.

That was not so easy, as she had already discovered. She was soon complaining to her mother that she was quite worn out. Not only was she harassed by the cares of running the household. She was often up all night with Charles and she had to endure his incessant demands, his possessiveness and his sudden rages. When he did try to do business his concentration was poor and he was so forgetful that he often found himself signing the wrong name at the end of documents; not surprisingly, perhaps, in view of his many previous pseudonyms. To make matters worse, no matter how weak or ill he felt, he never lost his taste for plays, the opera and ceremonial. He insisted on being carried out to such entertainments and of course Charlotte had to go too. He was more like a fifteen-year-old than a grown man, she remarked wearily.

It was a relief when he did agree to spend a day quietly in his apartments, sunk in thought or listening to music. He kept a piper and would ask him to play 'Lochaber No More'. When he heard the mournful highland lament, the tears came to his eyes. Occasionally, he felt well enough to play his own set of bagpipes and sometimes he enjoyed the companionship of a musical friend. When Domenico

Corri, the famous harpsichordist, came to call on him, he would get out his cello and they would perform duets together.

His few visitors had to be selected with care, of course. There was one unfortunate occasion when a stranger arrived and announced himself as the Count of Vaudreuil. This was the son of the very man who had arrested Charles in Paris before his expulsion from France. As soon as he heard the dreaded name, the old man fainted. Another evening, an English caller questioned him too persistently about the sufferings of the Jacobites after Culloden. He collapsed, and when Charlotte came hurrying to the rescue she exclaimed reproachfully to the visitor, 'Oh Sir, what is this? You must have been speaking to my father about Scotland and the highlanders. No one dares to mention these subjects in his presence!' Even after more than forty years, some memories were too painful to be borne.

Charlotte herself was mortally ill now with a liver disease. Her motives in coming to her father had been largely mercenary, but she was kind and she had brought him a measure of comfort. For two years he lived on in her care, becoming increasingly difficult and increasingly confused, while she longed for her French family and regretted her seemingly interminable exile. Eventually, not long after his sixty-seventh birthday, Charles suffered a stroke and on 31 January 1788 he finally slipped away.

The Pope refused to allow him to be given a royal funeral in St Peter's and so he was buried in his brother's cathedral at Frascati. Charlotte stayed on in Rome afterwards, trying to settle his estate, but less than two years later she died of cancer. She left her mother a handsome pension but Clementina Walkinshaw did not long enjoy her

198. Replica of Charles's death mask.
(On loan to the Scottish National Portrait Gallery from Duddingston Preservation Society)

199. *George IV* by
T. Lawrence.
(Scottish National Portrait
Gallery)

increased comfort. She was forced to flee from Paris during the French Revolution and she ended her days in Switzerland, in great poverty.

Charlotte's two daughters apparently failed to survive childhood, but her son, Charles Edward, grew up to be a soldier. Although twice married, he had no children and since he showed little interest in politics he was allowed to tour Britain, visiting the scenes of his grandfather's campaign. With his death in 1854, Charles's direct line ended. Tales of children born of his marriage to Louise of Stolberg were mere fantasy.

The Stuart cause itself had been over for many years. Cardinal York certainly styled himself 'Henry IX' but it was an empty title and everyone knew it. He lost most of his money in the French Revolution and when the invading French army sacked his palace the British government came to his rescue. They saw that he reached the safety of Venice, where George III sent him a generous gift of money.

Eventually he was able to return to Frascati and there he died in 1807, bequeathing to George III's eldest son those few British crown jewels still in Stuart possession. His body was taken to Rome for burial and the Pope agreed that his brother's coffin should go too. Charles and Henry now lie beside their father in St Peter's. Above them is a handsome marble monument. It was placed there at the instigation of the Prince Regent, the future King George IV of Great Britain. The houses of Stuart and Hanover had been reconciled at last.

200. The tomb of James III, Charles and Henry, by A. Canova, in St Peter's, Rome. Charles's features are on the right, with Henry in the middle and their father on the left. (Photograph, Vatican Museums)

FURTHER READING

Prince Charles was the subject of much interest during his own lifetime and many of those who knew him set down their version of events or told it to friends. The shorter narratives are to be found in *Origins of the 'Forty Five* edited by W B Blaikie (Scottish History Society 1975), and in the three volumes of *The Lyon in Mourning* edited by Henry Paton and reprinted by the Scottish History Society in 1975, along with Blaikie's invaluable *Itinerary of Prince Charles Edward Stuart*.

Longer descriptions appear as separate books: Colonel O'Sullivan's reminiscences, for example, are preserved in *1745 and after* edited by Alistair and Henrietta Tayler (London 1938), and Lord Elcho's story features in *A Short Account of the Affairs of Scotland in the Years 1744, 1745, 1746* edited by Evan Charteris (Edinburgh 1907). His unpublished journal, in French, is in a private collection and formed the basis for a memoir in the same volume. Charles Wogan's tale of Clementina's escape from Innsbruck is printed in its original French, in *Narratives of the Detention, Liberation and Marriage of Maria Clementina Stuart* edited by John T Gilbert and published by Irish University Press in 1970.

Among the many relevant histories and biographies, the best are still John Home's careful and elegantly written *The History of the Rebellion in the Year 1745* (London 1802) and Andrew Lang's entertaining *Prince Charles Edward Stuart* (London 1900). The most recent writers include Bruce Lenman, whose *Jacobite Risings in Britain 1689–1748* (London 1980) and other works are strongly critical of the Prince, while F J McLynn, *France and the Jacobite Rising of 1745* (Edinburgh 1981) and *The Jacobite Army in England 1745* (Edinburgh 1983) is sympathetic to him.

On specific topics, John S Gibson's excellent *Ships of the '45: The Rescue of the Young Pretender* (London 1967) explores the naval aspect of the campaign, and L L Bongie's *The Love of a Prince* (Vancouver 1986) is a scholarly examination of Charles's relationship with his cousin Louise. Professor Bongie promises a sequel on the Princess of Talmont. *Highland Songs of the Forty Five*, edited by John Lorne Campbell (Scottish Gaelic Text Society 1984) gives an intriguing insight into reactions at the time and the names and fates of the less well-known Jacobites are to be discovered in *Muster Rolls of Prince Charles Edward Stuart's Army 1745–46*, edited by Alistair Livingstone of Bachuil and others (Aberdeen 1984), and in *The Prisoners of the '45*, edited by B G Seton and J G Arnot (Scottish History Society 1928).

The Prince's final years in France and Italy are chronicled in Andrew Lang's *Pickle the Spy* (London 1897) and in Sir Horace Mann's reports, printed in *The Decline of the Last Stuarts* (London 1845). Henrietta Tayler provides colourful detail in *Prince Charlie's Daughter* (London 1950) and George Sherburn takes the story of the Jacobite Stuarts to its conclusion with *Roehenstart: A Late Stuart Pretender* (Chicago 1960), a biography of the Prince's grandson.